Improving Subject Teaching

In many countries, questions are being raised about the quality and value of educational research, and whether educational practice can ever draw upon research evidence as productively as in fields such as medicine. This book explores the relationship between research and practice in education, using the case of science education as an example. It looks at the extent to which current practice could be said to be *informed* by knowledge or ideas generated by research – and at the extent to which the use of current practices or the adoption of new ones are, or could be, supported by research evidence – and so be said to be *evidence-based*. The issues considered are not specific to science, but apply to the teaching and learning of any curriculum subject.

The book draws on the findings of four interrelated research studies, carried out by the Evidence-based Practice in Science Education (EPSE) Research Network. It considers:

- how research might be used to establish greater consensus about curriculum;
- how research can inform the design of assessment tools and teaching interventions;
- teachers' and other science educators' perceptions of the influence of research on their teaching practices and their students' learning;
- the extent to which evidence can show that an educational practice 'works'.

The book is unique in exploring the issues raised by the current debate about educational research within the context of the teaching and learning of a specific curriculum subject. Rather than looking at how research might inform educational practices in the abstract, it looks at how research can lead to improvement in the teaching of specific pieces of knowledge, or specific skills, that we value. The issues it explores are therefore of direct interest and relevance to educational practitioners and policy-makers.

Robin Millar is Professor of Science Education, University of York, UK. **John Leach** is Professor of Science Education, University of Leeds, UK. **Jonathan Osborne** is Professor of Science Education, King's College London, UK. **Mary Ratcliffe** is Professor of Science Education, University of Southampton, UK.

Improving Learning TLRP

Series Editor: Andrew Pollard, Director of the ESRC Teaching and Learning Programme

Improving Subject Teaching

Lessons from research in science education

Robin Millar, John Leach, Jonathan Osborne and Mary Ratcliffe

with Jaume Ametller, Hannah Bartholomew, Sue Collins, Rick Duschl, Vicky Hames, Andy Hind, Jenny Lewis and Phil Scott

Routledge
Taylor & Francis Group

LONDON AND NEW YORK

First published 2006
by Routledge
2 Park Square, Milton Park, Abingdon, Oxon OX14 4RN

Simultaneously published in the USA and Canada
by Routledge
270 Madison Ave, New York, NY 10016

Routledge is an imprint of the Taylor and Francis Group, an informa business

Typeset in Charter ITC and StoneSans by
Keystroke, Jacaranda Lodge, Wolverhampton
Printed and bound in Great Britain by
MPG Books Ltd, Bodmin

British Library Cataloguing in Publication Data
A catalogue record for this book is available from the British Library

Library of Congress Cataloging in Publication Data
A catalog record for this book has been requested

ISBN10: 0–415–36209–1 (hbk)
ISBN10: 0–415–36210–5 (pbk)

ISBN13: 978–0–415–36209–2 (hbk)
ISBN13: 978–0–415–36210–8 (pbk)

Contents

Illustrations

Figures

Tables

Contributors

Robin Millar is Professor of Science Education in the Department of Educational Studies at the University of York. He was Co-ordinator of the Research Network Towards Evidence-based Practice in Science Education (EPSE). He directed EPSE Project 1 and co-directed Project 4.

John Leach is Professor of Science Education in the Centre for Studies in Science and Mathematics Education (CSSME) at the University of Leeds, and Head of the School of Education. He was a core member of the Research Network Towards Evidence-based Practice in Science Education (EPSE). He directed EPSE Project 2 with Phil Scott, and co-directed Project 4.

Jonathan Osborne holds the Chair of Science Education at King's College London. He was a core member of the Research Network Towards Evidence-based Practice in Science Education (EPSE). He directed EPSE Project 3 with Mary Ratcliffe, and co-directed Project 4.

Mary Ratcliffe is Professor of Science Education in the School of Education at the University of Southampton. She was a core member of the Research Network Towards Evidence-based Practice in Science Education (EPSE). She directed EPSE Project 3 with Jonathan Osborne, and was lead co-director for Project 4.

Jaume Ametller is a Research Fellow in the Centre for Studies in Science and Mathematics Education (CSSME) at the University of Leeds. He worked on EPSE Project 2.

Hannah Bartholomew was a Research Officer in the School of Education at King's College London, working on phase 2 of EPSE

Project 3 and on Project 4. She is now a lecturer in mathematics education at the University of Auckland.

Sue Collins was a Research Officer in the School of Education at King's College London, working on phase 1 of EPSE Project 3. She is now a Senior Research Officer at the Institute of Education University of London.

Rick Duschl was the Chair of Science Education at King's College from 1998 to 2003 and is now a full professor at Rutgers University, New Jersey. He contributed to phase 1 of EPSE Project 3.

Vicky Hames was a Research Officer in the Department of Educational Studies at the University of York, working on EPSE Projects 1 and 4. She now teaches in a primary school in North Yorkshire.

Andy Hind was a Research Officer in the Centre for Studies in Science and Mathematics Education (CSSME) at the University of Leeds, working on EPSE Projects 2 and 4. He is now Head of Science at a comprehensive school in Leeds.

Jenny Lewis is a Senior Lecturer in Science Education in the Centre for Studies in Science and Mathematics Education (CSSME) at the University of Leeds. She worked on EPSE Project 2.

Phil Scott is Professor of Science Education in the Centre for Studies in Science and Mathematics Education (CSSME) at the University of Leeds. He directed EPSE Project 2 with John Leach.

Series editor's preface

The Improving Learning series showcases findings from projects within ESRC's Teaching and Learning Research Programme (TLRP) – the UK's largest ever coordinated educational research initiative.

Books in the Improving Learning series are explicitly designed to support 'evidence-informed' decisions in educational practice and policy-making. In particular, they combine rigorous social and educational science with high awareness of the significance of the issues being researched.

Working closely with practitioners, organisations and agencies covering all educational sectors, the Programme has supported many of the UK's best researchers to work on the direct improvement of policy and practice to support learning. Over sixty projects have been supported, covering many issues across the lifecourse. We are proud to present the results of this work through books in the Improving Learning series.

Each book provides a concise, accessible and definitive *overview* of innovative findings from a TLRP investment. If more advanced information is required, the books may be used as a gateway to academic journals, monographs, websites, etc. On the other hand, shorter summaries and research briefings on key findings are also available via the Programme's website at www.tlrp.org.

We hope that you will find that the analysis and findings presented in this book are helpful to you in your work on improving outcomes for learners.

Andrew Pollard
Director, Teaching and Learning Research Programme
Institute of Education University of London

Preface

The research reported in this book has been carried out at a time when the quality of educational research is under intense scrutiny. Questions have been asked about its value to practitioners and policy makers in guiding them in the choices and decisions that they inevitably have to make. We approach these issues as researchers, but also with many years' experience of teaching, teacher education and curriculum development. We are personally convinced that research in the area we know best (science education) has produced knowledge, in the form of specific research findings and other more analytical and theoretical insights, that could, if more widely and systematically applied, lead to significant improvements in students' learning and attitudes. But equally we know that much practice takes little obvious account of knowledge generated by research, and that the evidence to back up our conviction that research could drive improvement is often less complete or compelling than we would wish. The work reported in this book stems from a desire to understand better the interface between research and practice in the context of the teaching and learning of a core subject of the school curriculum. Understanding better what research can provide, how we might 'engineer' improvements that draw significantly on research and test these in practice, and how potential users of the knowledge and insights generated by research view, understand and access research, are all necessary steps towards 'research evidence-based' or 'research evidence-informed' practice. In this book, we approach these issues from the perspective of one curriculum subject – science. They are not, however, specific to science education, but apply equally to the teaching of any curriculum subject. We therefore hope that all readers with an interest in the role of educational research will be able to see links to issues and questions in which they are interested.

This book is based on the work of the Evidence-based Practice in Science Education (EPSE) Research Network, funded by the UK Economic and Social Research Council (ESRC) in Phase 1 of the Teaching and Learning Research Programme (TLRP). The EPSE Network undertook four interrelated projects. Summaries of these can be found in the Appendix at the end of the book. In the body of the book, we have not set out to provide brief accounts of each project in turn. Instead, our aim is to draw selectively on the work undertaken by the EPSE Research Network to explore a number of general issues and themes about the actual (and potential) role of research in improving the way any subject of the school curriculum is taught and learned.

Part I

What is the issue?

Chapter 1

Research and practice in education

Education research is often criticised for having little impact on practice or policy. This book looks at the influence of research on the teaching of a curriculum subject. It asks what research can offer practitioners and policy makers in making choices and decisions about how a curriculum subject should be taught – and considers how research might need to change to influence practice in subject teaching more strongly. In this opening chapter, we try to disentangle two issues: the role of research in the design of teaching, and the extent to which research can provide a warrant (or justification) for teaching something in one way rather than another. We also summarise some of the key ideas and claims in the recent debate about the role and quality of education research, looking in particular at the suggestion that research in medicine and health provides a model for education research to follow.

Introduction

The past decade has seen a growing demand, in many countries, that education should become more 'evidence-based' – that is, that research should provide evidence to inform choices and decisions about educational matters. This demand has come particularly from those involved in educational policy making, and is part of a wider debate about the quality of public services in general, and the role of research in informing the decisions which practitioners and policy makers must inevitably make (Davies *et al.* 2000). Research, it is argued, provides a

Authored by Robin Millar, John Leach, Jonathan Osborne and Mary Ratcliffe

better basis for choice and action than tradition or 'professional wisdom'. It can challenge ineffective current practices; and provides a means of testing innovations so that only those which are seen to be effective are widely implemented. As David Blunkett, speaking in 2000 as Secretary of State for Education and Employment in the UK, put it:

> We need to be able to rely on . . . social scientists to tell us what works and why and what types of policy initiatives are likely to be most effective.
>
> (Blunkett 2000: 2)

This is very much the policy maker's perspective. How does the research–practice interface look from the viewpoint of the practitioner? Most teachers spend most of their working lives teaching a subject, or group of subjects. Most of the decisions that teachers routinely take are about the detail of how to plan and implement lessons that develop their students' ideas, skills and attitudes within a subject area. If educational research is to have an impact on practice, and be seen to have an impact, it is decisions of this sort that it must influence. Hence, it is on this issue, of the current influence of research on teachers' everyday practice and how it might be increased, that we want to focus in this book. Our reason for starting from the practitioner's perspective is not that we think the role of research in informing policy is less important. Far from it. But research-informed policy can only mean support and encouragement of practices that have themselves been shown to be soundly conceived and effective when implemented. The key questions, then, which we want to explore in this book might be summarised as follows:

- What contribution can research make to improving the teaching and learning of a school curriculum subject?
- Can research help us to improve the way subjects are taught, and the learning that ensues?
- If so, what kind of help can we reasonably expect research to provide: new information, perspectives or insights that we may need to consider and take into account; or clear and compelling evidence that certain interventions 'work' or do not?
- How should research be designed and carried out if it is to provide the kind of knowledge that can lead to practical improvements?

We will approach these questions from the perspective of one curriculum subject – science. The issues which they raise are not, however, specific to science education. They apply equally to the teaching of any curriculum subject. We have chosen to focus on science because that is the subject we know best. But it is only an example. We hope that readers who are interested in the teaching and learning of other subjects will be able to relate the discussion to their interests.

To argue that the teaching and learning of science (or of any other curriculum subject) should become more 'evidence-based' implies that research is capable of generating knowledge that makes possible the more effective teaching of specific bodies of knowledge and the skills and attitudes associated with them. The aim of this book is to explore critically the extent to which such a view can be sustained, identify the conditions which would have to be met to make it possible, and explore its strengths and limitations as a strategy for improving practice. The book arises from the work of the Evidence-based Practice in Science Education (EPSE) Research Network, funded by the UK Economic and Social Research Council (ESRC) within the Teaching and Learning Research Programme (TLRP). In the original research proposal, the Network's title was 'Towards evidence-based practice in science education'. That 'towards' is important despite its subsequent omission from the Network's shorthand name; indeed the title should perhaps be read with a question mark at the end. The aim of the Network was to improve our understanding of the interface between science education research and practice, and to explore what might be involved in moving school science education towards forms of practice that might be termed more 'evidence-based'. To this end, the Network undertook four projects, which are interrelated and were carried out in parallel rather than sequentially:

Project 1: Exploring the impact on teachers' practices, and student learning, of providing diagnostic tools informed by previous research on student learning.

Project 2: Developing and evaluating short teaching sequences that are explicitly informed by research evidence.

Project 3: Establishing the extent of 'expert' agreement on what people should know about the nature of scientific knowledge and the procedures of scientific enquiry, and exploring the practical implications of trying to teach the ideas seen as most important.

Project 4: Documenting and analysing science education practitioners' views on the actual and potential influence of research on their everyday practices.

Summaries of each of these projects are presented in the Appendix. Our intention in this book, however, is not simply to report and discuss the findings and outcomes of each in turn, but to use them together to explore a number of general issues and themes about the nature of research evidence in education and its relationship to practice.

Research, evidence and practice

To explore systematically the relationships between research and practice, and the ideas of 'evidence-based' or 'evidence-informed' practice, we need to clarify some terms, and develop a framework for exploring systematically the relationship between evidence (or knowledge) and practical choices and decisions. The task of developing and testing a comprehensive model of the complex interrelationships between research and practice is beyond the scope of this book. What we need is a model that is 'good enough' to provide a framework for discussion of the issues.

First, though, a word about the two terms 'evidence' and 'practice'. To call for education to become 'evidence-based' seems to imply that current practices are not based on 'evidence'. This is clearly untenable if taken literally: any rational human activity that involves participants in making choices and decisions clearly requires them to draw on past experience and learning – that is, on evidence. The issue is the kind, and the quality, of the evidence that is used. 'Evidence' in the phrase 'evidence-based education' clearly means 'evidence produced by research', that is, evidence collected through a systematic process of data collection and analysis, open to public scrutiny and, in principle at least, replicable by anyone who chooses to do so.

It is also worth clarifying what we mean by 'practice'. The phrase 'evidence-based practice' treats 'practice' as though it were a single category. But in reality, there are many different kinds of educational 'practices' that we might wish to make more 'evidence-based'. Some concern general aspects of school organisation and procedure (such as decisions about class size, or about expenditure on books compared to that on computers). Others are about teaching approaches that could be applied across all subjects (such as using formative assessment) or across all topics within a subject (such as the use of small-group practical work in science). These are 'practices' that a school or a department might choose to adopt in place of other alternatives. At a more content-specific level, there are the practices that a teacher or a school department follows in teaching specific topics (for example, the teaching scheme and materials used for teaching elementary electric circuit theory in lower secondary school) or even specific key ideas (such as the model of a chemical reaction as a rearrangement of atoms into new combinations).

A critical feature of all of these kinds of practices except the first (general aspects of school organisation and procedure) is that *content matters*. In other words, the quality of the decisions and choices made depends not only on general principles and criteria (perhaps deriving from some kind of theoretical position or analysis) but also on knowledge of and about the specific content being taught. This is clearly so for content-specific practices but is also true of generic practices that can be applied across subjects or across topics within a subject, such as formative assessment. These can only be implemented in the context of teaching some specific content – and the success or failure of the resulting practice will depend not only on the validity of the generic principle *per se* but also on how it is implemented with the chosen content. Again the decisions and choices involved depend on knowledge of and about that content. It is largely for this reason that we believe it essential to consider issues of 'evidence-based practice' from the perspective of the teaching of a specific subject.

How then might we begin to model the relationships between research evidence and practice? A central element of any such model is the knowledge base on which teachers draw in making decisions and choices. Research and informal experience both suggest that this includes a range of types of knowledge, acquired from a variety of sources (e.g. Brown and McIntyre 1993; Loughran 1999). The categories of teachers' professional knowledge identified in Figure 1.1 are based on the widely-used typology proposed by Shulman (1986, 1987). Many of these categories consist of both explicit (or declarative) knowledge – things a person could tell you that they know – and tacit knowledge, which cannot be fully expressed in words but is implicit in actions.

Teachers' professional knowledge comes from a variety of sources. Some of the more important ones are shown on the right-hand side of Figure 1.1. These are not, of course, as separate or distinct as this might seem to imply. For example, whilst a teacher may have direct knowledge of a specific research finding, the influence of research on his or her thinking may also be indirect. For instance, a teaching session in an initial or in-service teacher education programme might have been based on a specific research finding, or a general perspective that comes from research, as might the treatment of a topic in a textbook or a teaching resource. These may then influence a teacher's knowledge and

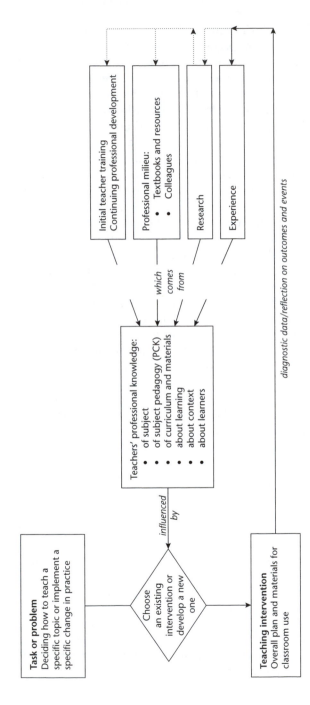

Figure 1.1 Influences on teachers' decision making

ideas, even though he or she may not recognise or acknowledge any specific research input. The dotted arrows on the right of Figure 1.1 try to represent this kind of indirect influence of research.

This complex professional knowledge base then influences the decisions that a teacher takes in deciding how to teach a specific topic or implement a specific change in some aspect of their practice. One possibility is that the teacher identifies an 'off the shelf', ready-made teaching scheme or set of teaching resources, and chooses to adopt this. This might be a published scheme or one that has been developed by a school department. It may be informed to a greater or lesser extent by research evidence. For example, the innovative short course, *Cognitive Acceleration through Science Education (CASE)* (Adey *et al.* 1996), is explicitly based on theoretical perspectives arising from research. On the other hand, recent research in the US would suggest that many school science textbooks are not significantly influenced by research findings (Kesidou and Roseman 2002). The extent of research influence may not be apparent to teachers choosing a particular intervention. And, even if they know that an intervention has been (or claims to be) informed by research, they may not be able to say what the primary research evidence is or how it has influenced the intervention. In the UK, choosing a published science teaching scheme or materials as the basis of a two- or three-year teaching programme has become increasingly common since the introduction of the national curriculum. In other countries, choosing a published 'programme' may also be the commonest way of tackling the kind of task or problem outlined in Figure 1.1.

The other possibility is that the teacher develops his or her own teaching intervention, perhaps selecting elements from a range of published materials and resources, and adapting or augmenting these using ideas from colleagues, or from initial or in-service training courses, or devised by the teacher himself or herself. Again this is quite common in UK schools. In this case, the teacher is drawing on many aspects of his or her professional knowledge, which has in turn come from some or all of the sources identified on the right-hand side of Figure 1.1. He or she may know of, or seek out, specific research findings that bear on the particular task in hand, and make considered use of these. Research findings may also have influenced the form and content of the teaching materials consulted, and used or adapted in developing the intervention – though this may or may not be recognised by the teacher in choosing to use them.

It follows that teaching interventions cannot be easily or sensibly divided into the categories 'research evidence-informed' and 'not research evidence-informed'. This would become even more apparent were we to go on to consider the implemented intervention rather than just the intended (or planned) intervention. A further raft of choices and decisions is involved in implementing any intervention, many of which have to be taken in the heat of the moment in the classroom. Rather, 'research evidence-informed' is a matter of degree – of the extent of influence of ideas and findings from research, and the 'quality' of this influence. Any given example of practice might therefore be regarded as more or less 'research evidence-informed'.

Finally, there is another, and somewhat different, sense in which a teacher's practice might be said to be 'evidence-informed'. This is where a teacher collects data on students' learning, or responses to an intervention more generally, as it proceeds, and uses this to help make decisions about what to do next. This might be done formally, as a piece of action research, or less formally as part of normal practice. The feedback loop in Figure 1.1 is an attempt to include within the model the kind of knowledge that can come from diagnostic assessment and critical reflection on practice.

Calling a practice 'research evidence-informed' is therefore making a claim about its design. In contrast to this, we propose to call a practice 'research evidence-based' if it has been implemented and evaluated, and there is evidence of some kind, based on data that have been systematically collected and analysed, and are available for public inspection, to support the view that it achieves all (or at least some) of its intended outcomes – and perhaps that it achieves these better than some other approach (Figure 1.2). This parallels usage in medicine and health, where calling a practice 'evidence-based' is also making a claim about its outcomes. In the medical context, such a claim is only likely to be made if the evidence comes from a *randomised controlled trial* (RCT, see p. 13) or, better still, a synthesis of several RCTs. Figure 1.2, however, does not specify that any particular research strategy or research design be used to evaluate a teaching intervention, in order to support the claim that using it is an instance of 'research evidence-based practice'. The research design used to evaluate a particular intervention may, of course, have a very significant bearing on the *strength* of the evidence of its outcomes – and hence on the justification for recommending that it be used more widely. These are issues to which we will return in the concluding chapter.

We are not attempting to claim that our proposed usage of the terms 'evidence-informed' and 'evidence-based' is the 'correct' one. We recognise that these terms have been used with a variety of meanings,

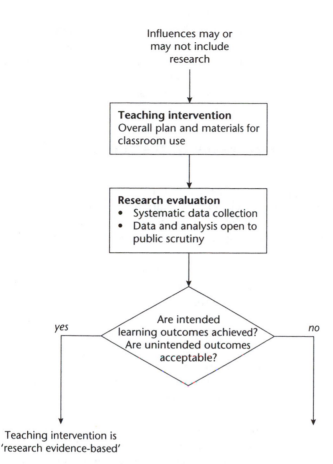

Figure 1.2 Research evidence-based practice

often indeed almost interchangeably. Rather we want to make the point that there are two distinct ideas here, both of which are important. One is about the extent to which the *design* of a teaching intervention is influenced by research findings or ideas; the other is about the extent to which research has provided evidence about the *outcomes* of the intervention, and hence a warrant for choosing to use it. Not only are these distinctly different, they are also independent. It is possible for a teaching intervention that is 'research evidence-informed' not to have been formally evaluated and shown to 'work'. Indeed, it is common. But it is also possible for a teaching intervention that is not to any great extent informed by research, perhaps because it is based largely on pragmatic or 'commonsense' considerations, to be evaluated systematically and shown to achieve its objectives – and hence to be regarded as an example of 'research evidence-based practice'. An intervention could, of course, be both. By using terms consistently in the way we propose, it may be possible to keep these issues more clearly distinct. In this book we are interested in both.

Improving subject teaching: The role of research

This section explores the more general debate about the nature and value of educational research, and the relationship between educational research and practice – a debate that has been going on over the past decade in the UK and elsewhere. We see this book as a contribution to that debate.

The growing emphasis on 'evidence-based practice' in the public services referred to on the first page of this chapter has emerged at a time when the quality of educational research and its practical usefulness are being seriously questioned in many countries. In the UK, the Teacher Training Agency (TTA) lecture in 1996 by Professor David Hargreaves initiated a debate that still continues. Hargreaves asked if teaching could be said to be a research-based profession, and concluded that it could not. The problem, he argued, lay in the nature and quality of the outcomes of educational research:

> Given the huge amounts of educational research conducted over the past fifty years or more, there are few areas which have yielded a corpus of research evidence regarded as scientifically sound and as a worthwhile resource to guide professional action.
>
> (Hargreaves 1996: 2)

Reviews of educational research for the UK Office for Standards in Education (OfSTED) (Tooley and Darby 1998) and the Department for Education and Employment (DfEE) (Hillage et al. 1998) reinforced this view that the outcomes of educational research rarely provide useful guidance for policy makers or practitioners and that, as a result, 'the actions and decisions of policy-makers are insufficiently informed by research' (Hillage et al. 1998: xi).

Turning to the question of how the quality of educational research might be improved, Hargreaves drew a comparison with medical research, and the growing emphasis on evidence-based medicine. First, he noted that:

> In medicine, as in the natural sciences, research has a broadly cumulative character. Research projects seek explicitly to build on earlier research – by confirming or falsifying it, by extending or refining it, by replacing it with better evidence or theory, and so on. Most educational research is, by contrast, non-cumulative. . . . A few small-scale investigations of an issue produce inconclusive and contestable findings of little practical relevance.
>
> (Hargreaves 1996: 2)

A second important difference, Hargreaves claimed, lay in the identity of the people carrying out the research: the involvement of practising doctors in medical research, including setting the research agenda, ensured that the outcomes were relevant to practice. In contrast, educational research is carried out mainly by academics who are no longer directly involved in the educational practices they are researching, so it risks becoming 'a private, esoteric activity, seen as irrelevant by most practitioners' (ibid. p. 3). Third, Hargreaves saw 'a very sharp difference in the way the two professions approach applied research. Much medical research is not itself basic research . . . but a type of applied research which gathers evidence about what works in what circumstances' (ibid. p. 2).

Not surprisingly, many of the points raised in Hargreaves's lecture and in the reviews by Hillage et al. and by Tooley and Darby were challenged by other educational researchers (for example, Edwards 1996; Gray 1996; Norris 1996). Hammersley (1997) accepted Hargreaves's criticism that educational research has not led to a cumulative growth of knowledge – as, it seems, do many educational researchers in the UK (Taylor 2002). He questioned, however, whether clinical medicine offers a useful model for educational research to follow, arguing that the problems of generating knowledge about education are considerable and stem from the nature of educational knowledge (and social knowledge more generally). Essentially, the issue is whether law-like generalisations about educational practices, even of a probabilistic nature, exist and can be found by careful research.

Persuasive – and highly influential – arguments for the use of *randomised controlled trials* in educational research have, however, been advanced by others sympathetic to Hargreaves's analysis of the limitations of educational research (e.g. Fitz-Gibbon 2000; Tymms and Fitz-Gibbon 2002). Slavin (2002), for example, argues that:

> Once we have dozens or hundreds of randomized or carefully matched experiments going on each year on all aspects of educational practice, we will begin to make steady, irreversible progress. Until then, we are merely riding the pendulum of educational fashion.
>
> (p. 19)

RCTs can also help to identify and exclude innovations that are worthless or damaging. Torgerson and Torgerson (2001), for example, claim that:

> There are undoubtedly some educational innovations which are harmful to the educational prospects of children. Without testing them in robust trials we simply do not know what is helpful and what is downright detrimental.
>
> (p. 323)

These are not new ideas, but ones with a long history in the field of education (Bain 1879). There are, however, few examples of trials which have had a marked influence on educational practice or policy. And there is also an important counter-argument, with an equally long history, which questions the very notion of a 'science of education', and argues that research in social settings (including education) should not seek universal generalisations, because these do not and cannot exist, but rather to illuminate and interpret events from the perspectives of those involved (Parlett and Hamilton 1972) – as the social context, which is often unique, is a major determinant of individuals' actions.

A debate about the quality and direction of educational research, similar to that in the UK, has also been going on over the past decade in the United States. Here the advocates of evidence-based education, based upon the findings of randomised controlled trials (Boruch 1997; Mosteller and Boruch 2002; Slavin 2002), have made more striking inroads into national policy. The No Child Left Behind Act (US Congress 2001), which currently dominates educational discussion in the United States, mentions 'scientifically based research' 110 times. It defines 'scientifically based research' as 'rigorous, systematic and objective procedures to obtain valid knowledge' which includes research that 'is evaluated using experimental or quasi-experimental designs', preferably with random assignment (Slavin, 2002: 15).

A specific target of the US Department of Education (2002) *Strategic Plan for 2002–2007* is that, from 2004, seventy-five per cent of the research projects funded by the Department of Education to explore 'causal questions' should use randomised experimental designs. (By 'causal questions', they mean those which ask if a specific factor, such as the use of a specific teaching intervention, correlates with, and therefore possibly causes, a given outcome.) Other actions include setting up the *What Works Clearinghouse* (2003) 'to provide educators, policymakers, researchers and the public with a central and trusted source of scientific evidence of what works in education', and commissioning a 'user friendly guide' on educational research which includes a 'checklist to use in evaluating whether an intervention is backed by rigorous evidence' (US Department of Education 2003). Here 'rigorous' is synonymous with 'obtained from an experimental trial'. The National Research Council report *Scientific Inquiry in Education* (Shavelson and Towne 2002) can be seen as an attempt to defend a broader definition of 'scientific research' in education, which recognises the diversity of educational questions that might be investigated empirically and the range of research methods and designs that might be therefore regarded as 'scientific'.

Research designs for evaluating subject teaching

Given the prevalence of comparisons between educational research and medical research, it may be useful to say a little about the idea of 'evidence-based medicine' and the view of research on which it is based. Sackett *et al.* (1996) define evidence-based medicine as:

> The conscientious, explicit and judicious use of current best evidence in making decisions about the care of individual patients. The practice of evidence-based medicine means integrating individual clinical expertise with the best available external clinical evidence from systematic research.

> (p. 71)

They are careful to make clear that this is not '"cookbook" medicine' (p. 72); professional expertise and judgement have an important role. The aim is that doctors' decisions about the treatment of individual patients should, where possible, be based on evidence that the prescribed treatment is likely to lead to better outcomes than other alternatives. Gray (2002) calls this 'evidence-based decision making' and contrasts it with 'opinion-based decision making', where doctors' actions follow established or traditional ways of proceeding, or personal preferences based on individual experience.

In many areas of medicine, the accepted method for obtaining trustworthy evidence, on which decisions can safely be based, is the *clinical trial* – an experimental comparison of two (or more) treatments in which patients are allocated randomly to groups, each of which receives one of the treatments. The numbers of successful and unsuccessful outcomes in each group are then compared, using standard statistical methods, to assess the significance of any differences observed. The use of RCTs in medicine has its origins in trials of the efficacy of drug-based treatments. By allocating patients randomly to the treatment and control groups, the influence of other factors (both those we might anticipate and those we might not suspect) is eliminated – so that any observed difference can safely be attributed to the difference in treatment.

The application of this approach to evaluate educational interventions designed to inform or improve subject teaching, however, immediately raises some issues and questions. First, medical treatments are normally applied to individuals, whereas educational ones are typically applied to whole classes. This can be addressed by treating the class as the 'unit' that is allocated randomly to the 'treatment' or control group. One consequence, however, is to increase substantially the number of individuals who have to be involved in a study, in order to obtain clear evidence that an intervention does or does not have an effect. Second, and perhaps more importantly, subject teaching interventions are much more complex than treatments that simply involve taking a tablet (or having an injection) at regular intervals for a specified period of time. They are therefore more difficult to specify completely (to say exactly what the intervention is, so that it can be implemented reasonably consistently by different people in different places), and the outcomes are more difficult to measure. This issue is explored through specific examples in the second section of Part II (Chapters 5–7) of this book.

It should, however, also be acknowledged that many medical interventions are more complex than drug-based treatments. As the RCT has become established in medicine as the 'gold standard' for research evidence, trials have been used or proposed to evaluate a wide range of types of intervention, including strategies for modifying health professionals' behaviour, community-based health programmes, forms of individual and group therapy, and health and sex education programmes. These are referred to in the medical research literature as 'complex interventions' (Campbell *et al.* 2000). If an analogy is to be drawn between medical research and research designed to inform or improve subject teaching, then in most cases the appropriate parallel is with 'complex interventions' in medicine, rather than with drug-based treatments.

Measurement of outcomes also poses significantly greater problems for subject teaching interventions than for many medical ones. For many medical interventions, the desired outcome is either the patient's survival for a given period, or recovery to 'normal' health. Davies (1999) argues that medical outcomes are not all as simple as this, and are often less straightforward to measure than might be supposed. But his conclusion that there is little difference in this respect between medicine and education is less than persuasive, when considered in the context of research designed to inform or improve subject teaching. Whereas medical interventions have an essentially convergent set of outcomes, aiming to take the individual from a 'deficit state' (illness) towards an agreed and identifiable 'normal state' (health), subject teaching interventions aim to take individuals from a 'normal state' to an 'enhanced state' in which their knowledge, or skills, or attitudes have been extended or developed in some way. An initial temptation is to assume that it is easy to specify enhanced knowledge outcomes that are desirable, but agreeing upon such outcomes and how they might be measured is actually far from straightforward, as we will show in Chapters 2 and 3. Furthermore, subject teaching aims to engender motivation and enjoyment amongst students, and it is hard to argue that an intervention has succeeded if it has a negative effect on motivation, irrespective of knowledge outcomes. There are clearly many forms of 'enhancement' – and correspondingly many ways of attempting to measure and assess the extent to which they are realised. We explore this issue through examples of subject teaching in Chapters 5–7. This difficulty of specifying outcomes calls into question the usefulness of the 'treatment' metaphor when thinking about educational interventions. It also draws attention to the critical importance of a sound and persuasive outcome measure. This is necessary to help clarify and define the outcome we are seeking, as well as to measure the extent to which it is achieved.

The RCT is not, however, the only research design that has been advocated in recent debates about the quality of educational research. Another much discussed approach is the 'design experiment'. This has its origins in the work of Brown (1992) and Collins (1993). Rather than using clinical medicine as a model, an analogy is drawn with engineering practice. An educational intervention (such as a teaching scheme for addressing a particular area of a subject) is seen as an engineered 'artefact', designed to solve a particular problem or accomplish a particular task. Ultimately it will be judged a success (or a failure) on the basis of how well it works in the contexts in which it is used. Typically, the development process involves iterative improvement. Starting from an initial prototype, the artefact evolves in stages, through a series of investigations which may alternate between field settings (to see how it works *in situ*) and laboratory settings (to test specific aspects under more controlled conditions). The final goal is not a tightly defined, prescriptive intervention, but rather a design 'template' that can be used to generate interventions that 'work' in a variety of settings. In the process, the theoretical ideas that underpinned the development of the prototype are also challenged, refined and extended. So the outcome is not only a design for artefacts that 'work', but also new (or improved) educational knowledge.

One attraction of the design experiment approach is that it is clearly more useful to show that certain design features or criteria 'work', than that any one intervention based upon them does. It also offers a model of the research-practice interface in which professional insight, engagement and reflection have a central role. For these reasons, design experiments are well-suited to studies of the effectiveness of approaches to subject teaching. Indeed, it is difficult to imagine how an RCT could be designed (or resourced) to test the relative effectiveness of two detailed approaches to teaching a particular piece of subject content, as we illustrate in Chapter 5.

However, the precise nature of a design experiment, and the features which characterise the approach, are often unclear in articles written about the approach. Whilst this kind of methodological flexibility has some advantages, it is also a potential weakness. Gorard (2004), for example, comments that:

> many design experiments have been conducted by advocates of particular approaches or artefacts. . . . This makes it an especial concern that so few of their reports make any mention of comparison or control groups. Without these, and without working towards a definitive test, how can they persuade others that they have successfully eliminated rival explanations?
>
> (pp. 106–7)

This brings us back to the issue of outcomes, how we measure them, and how we evaluate and judge the significance of the results we obtain.

Whereas the results of an RCT can be logically compelling, those of a design experiment are likely to be more open to interpretation – and hence may be less likely to persuade people to change practices or policies. These are issues to which we will return later in the book.

Improving school science

Although this book is primarily concerned with general issues about the relationship between educational research on the one hand, and practice and policy on the other, the research which it reports and discusses is on the teaching and learning of science at school level. It may therefore be useful to say briefly what we consider to be the aspects of school science education that are currently a cause of concern and which therefore stand in greatest need of improvement – to set in context the research studies we go on to discuss in the remainder of this book. It might be expected that the issues that concern science educators would vary widely from country to country. In fact, there is a remarkable level of agreement. We would highlight in particular the following:

- In many countries there is a concern about the falling numbers of students who choose to study science beyond the age when it is a compulsory element of the curriculum. This is seen as having social and economic implications for the future.
- The falling enrolment in more advanced science courses is seen as a reflection of the disaffection of many students, during the compulsory phase of education, with science as a subject. Studies in many countries reveal negative attitudes towards the subject, and declining interest in it from early secondary school age onwards. Science is seen as difficult, as offering little scope for imagination or creativity, and as not valuing students' own views and ideas.
- Students in many countries report a disjunction between the science they are taught in schools and the more interesting science that they hear about on the television or read about in newspapers. Many educators recognise a need to orient school science for all pupils more strongly towards 'scientific literacy' – the kind of understanding that citizens require – rather than seeing it as a pre-professional training in the science disciplines.
- In order to deal sensibly with science-related issues that arise in everyday life, it is widely agreed that citizens need an understanding

of the nature of scientific knowledge and the processes of scientific enquiry, so that they may become more astute 'consumers' of scientific information. In most countries, however, learning goals in this area are not well defined or strongly emphasised. In particular, they are often not assessed, and hence are not prominent in teaching programmes.

- There is a growing awareness, in many countries, of the dilemma of trying to provide a science education that is appropriate for all future citizens whilst also catering adequately for the needs of those students who may choose to continue their study of science to more advanced levels. There are increasing doubts amongst science educators about the possibility of addressing adequately, within a single science curriculum, both 'scientific literacy' aims and those appropriate to the pre-professional training of future scientists.

- Research in many countries consistently shows that many students acquire little understanding of fundamental science concepts. Many retain their prior non-scientific ideas, or fail to integrate the taught ideas into a coherent framework. Most is quickly forgotten.

- Tests used to assess science performance, at all levels from schools to international surveys, are criticised for over-emphasising recall of discrete 'bits' of knowledge, rather than understanding of worthwhile ideas and fundamental concepts. Indeed, research has shown that students who score quite well on such tests often cannot give correct answers to questions probing their understanding of basic ideas.

These, then, are the sorts of issues on which science educators might look to research for assistance in solving, or at least ameliorating. Several are about values: what we ought to be trying to teach. These, it might be argued, are essentially non-empirical, though we will discuss in Chapter 2 (and to some extent in Chapter 3) how research might contribute to clarifying them, and helping to work towards better solutions. The other issues are about how best to achieve the goals we have chosen. Here research might reasonably be expected to offer guidance and assistance in improving practices and outcomes.

Overview of book

In this opening chapter, we have set out a framework for discussing and exploring the relationships between research evidence and practice, and explained the sense in which we will use the terms 'research evidence-informed practice' and 'research evidence-based practice' throughout this book. We have then presented a brief overview of the debate that has raged internationally over the past decade about the quality of educational research, and its usefulness to practitioners and policy makers, making some specific points about how this relates to issues concerning the teaching and learning *of a curriculum subject*.

We return to these issues in the final chapter, Chapter 9, drawing on the experience and outcomes of the four research projects we carried out to address the four questions identified at the beginning of Chapter 1. Chapter 9 considers the extent to which current practice in science education could be termed 'research evidence-informed' and 'research-evidence based', and asks what might be involved in seeking to make it more so. It also explores the implications of the aspiration to have more evidence-based practice: for the design and conduct of educational research, for the ways in which research is mediated to practitioners, and for the professionalism of teachers.

If Chapters 1 and 9 bracket the book, then chapters 2–8 are (to use another metaphor) 'the meat in the sandwich'. These report and discuss in detail some aspects of the four research projects we carried out. We have chosen not to report these projects sequentially – as they were not designed to be carried out in this way and were, in fact, undertaken in parallel. Rather we have tried to use them to draw out some more general issues about the relationships between research and practice, using examples from different projects to illustrate and explore these. Chapters 2–4 look at the role of research in addressing the question: what should we teach? Here the focus is on the role of research in informing the *design* of teaching. Chapter 2 explores how research might contribute more systematically to decisions about curriculum objectives. It discusses the use of the Delphi study method to establish the nature and extent of agreement within and between different 'expert groups'. Chapter 3 then looks at how research might inform the more detailed specification of learning outcomes, by exploring issues which arise in developing and using assessment items to 'measure' attainment of important learning outcomes. Finally, in this Part of the book, Chapter 4 discusses what is involved in designing sequences of lessons that draw clearly and explicitly on research. The focus of these chapters is therefore on the development of examples of 'research evidence-informed practice', as we have characterised it in this opening chapter.

Chapters 5–7 then ask: what can research tell us about the outcomes of teaching? These chapters consider three different examples of implementation and evaluation of specific teaching interventions, exploring the issues involved in collecting the kind of evidence that might support the claim that an intervention meets some, or all, of its objectives, and which might therefore justify recommending that others adopt it. Chapter 5 reports on the outcomes of a research evaluation of the teaching sequence whose development has been discussed in Chapter 4. Chapter 6 looks at the ways in which teachers' practices were modified and changed by providing them with access to the kinds of assessment tools discussed in Chapter 3 – and at the teachers' views on this, and on its impact on their students' learning. Chapter 7 then considers what might be involved for teachers in trying to teach some of the ideas which emerged as important curriculum objectives from the Delphi study discussed in Chapter 2. Chapters 5–7 therefore revisit the three projects discussed in Chapters 2–4, but now looking at *outcomes* of interventions, rather than issues about their design.

Chapter 8 then asks: what influences the impact of research on practice? In contrast to Chapters 2–7 which look at issues from the researchers' perspective, Chapter 8 considers the research–practice interface from the perspective of the practitioner. The chapter presents and discusses the outcomes of an interview and focus group study of the views of a large sample of teachers and other science education practitioners (such as textbook writers, examiners, and so on) on the influence of research on their day-to-day practice. It identifies the features of research which make it more (or less) persuasive to potential users, and some factors which seem to facilitate or hinder the influence of research on practice in the teaching of a specific subject. Chapter 9, as we have already said, then draws together insights from all four research projects to make some more general points about the research–practice interface.

Summary

Educational research is often seen as having relatively little impact on practice and policy. In exploring the relationship between research and practice, it is useful to distinguish between the notions of 'research evidence-informed practice' (meaning a practice whose design has been influenced by insights or findings from research) and 'research evidence-based practice' (meaning a practice for which there is evidence, from a research evaluation, that it 'works').

Some researchers have argued that research in medicine and health, centring on the use of randomised controlled trials to evaluate treatments and interventions, provides a model that education research should follow. Education differs from health, however, in the complexity of interventions and the clarity with which outcomes can be measured – and so other research designs, such as the design experiment, may be more appropriate. These issues are explored in subsequent chapters, through examples drawn from the four research projects undertaken by the Evidence-based Practice in Science Education (EPSE) Research Network.

Part II

What does the research tell us?

Chapter 2

Specifying curriculum goals

Less of an art, more of a science?

Is there a role for research in specifying curriculum objectives? It might seem that these are determined by our values and priorities, and not by empirical evidence. But research may nonetheless be useful in exploring the views of different key groups on curriculum objectives, and establishing the extent of agreement about these within and between groups. This chapter explores the contribution that research evidence might make to clarifying and informing decisions about curriculum objectives. The context is the strand of the science curriculum that deals with students' understanding *of science itself* (as distinct from developing their scientific knowledge of the natural world). This may appear subject-specific, but in fact the underlying issue is common to all curriculum subjects. It is the extent to which research evidence can inform decisions, at a macro-level of policy and planning, about the broad aims and goals of curricula.

Introduction

Broadly speaking, any curriculum in any subject area is an attempt by the stakeholders in a society to define the knowledge that the society considers significant. Common justifications for the inclusion of science in compulsory education are that such knowledge has utilitarian value or, alternatively, is of intrinsic worth. It is scientific knowledge, after all, that offers us the best explanations of the material world. Moreover, science offers us a range of methods for creating new knowledge and,

Authored by Jonathan Osborne, Mary Ratcliffe, Sue Collins and Rick Duschl

as 'way of knowing', is a major cultural referent which permeates contemporary life in the manner, for instance, that Shakespearean references pervade the English language. For all these reasons, therefore, an understanding of the basic rudiments of science is generally considered an essential part of the intellectual capital necessary to participate and function in contemporary society.

In the case of the science curriculum, discussion of its rationale and content has come to prominence in the past fifteen years because of the increasing recognition that science and technology are sufficiently important aspects of contemporary society and our cultural heritage that *all* students in England must be educated in science from age 5 to 16. In the past, the goals of the science curriculum were primarily determined by the needs of those select few who would continue their education in science post-16. But, as the rationale for science education has changed, questions have arisen about the kind of science that is appropriate for the majority of young people who will not continue with any study of science post-16, and about its goals.

The broad response to such questions has been an argument that science education should primarily be a preparation for citizenship, as compulsory science education can only be justified if it offers something of universal value to all (AAAS 1993, 1998; Millar and Osborne 1998). A corollary of this changing emphasis has been a broadening in the range of stakeholders who have a legitimate interest in determining the goals of the school science curriculum. No longer are decisions about the curriculum the sole preserve of scientists and teachers of science but now those individuals engaged in what is loosely termed 'science studies' and science communication also have a legitimate voice.

However, a problem inherent in the process of determining curriculum goals is that the criteria for selection are often unclear, and frequently the outcome of labyrinthine consultations with diverse stakeholders. Moreover, not all of these stakeholders carry equal weight. For instance, it is often the scientific community that plays a significant role in defining the major features of the domain. Those individuals who are charged with the process of formulating a curriculum have little, if any, empirical evidence to inform the process or contest powerful views. Hence, the final product may be a curriculum which is inappropriate to the needs and requirements of the society of the time, let alone the future. A consequence is that there are occasions when either the knowledge within the domain is contested, or a distorted emphasis is placed on selected components. Attempts to classify Darwin's theory of evolution in a number of states in the US as 'only a theory' are an example of the former, whilst the ongoing debate about the relative importance of content and process in science education is an example of the latter. Given the growing significance of science in contemporary society, it is somewhat surprising that the procedure of specifying curriculum goals has been somewhat less of a science and more of an art.

Teaching 'ideas about science'

The case for change in contemporary school science has been made by several authors, for instance, in the UK by Millar and Osborne (1998) and in the US by the American Association for the Advancement of Science (1993, 1998) and the National Research Council (1995). An essential argument in all of these reports is that, as well as addressing the specific content of science and its methods, any science education should also provide a better understanding of a set of 'ideas about science'. Commonly this phrase is used to refer to a basic philosophical understanding of the nature of science, the function and role of data in scientific argument, how the scientific community functions, the role of risk and its assessment, and the implications of science and technology for society. The case has been made that such knowledge is a critically important element of 'scientific literacy' both by people interested in the public understanding of science (including scientists, sociologists, philosophers of science) (Fuller 1997) and by science educators (Jenkins 1999).

Only recently has there been any attempt to develop a curriculum that is a reflection of such rationales. Rather, most science courses have been adapted from curricula whose roots lie in programmes that were essentially conceived as foundational studies for those who were to become the next generation of scientists. Despite notable attempts to broaden the view of science presented – for instance in the first version of the English national curriculum (DES 1989) or in the emphasis on teaching science as a process of inquiry in the American National Science Education Standards (National Research Council 1995) – curricula have tended to assimilate minimal elements of the nature of science through a process of accretion. For instance, the 1999 version of the English national curriculum (DfEE/QCA 1999) has a component termed *Ideas and Evidence* that, at the time of writing, accounts for a mere 5 per cent of the mark in all national examinations.

A basic problem confronting those charged with specifying any curriculum incorporating 'ideas about science' is that, whilst there is an emergent consensus about their value within the school science curriculum, there is less agreement about those elements that should be included. Within the domain of science, the 1990s have been characterised by a vigorous debate about the nature of science between scientists and the sociologists of science that has been dubbed the 'science wars'. For instance, scientists commonly tend to perceive the nature of the scientific enterprise from a critical realist perspective that sees the production of knowledge as leading to a closer knowledge of reality. In contrast, the case has been made by sociologists and others that social practices and cultural influences shape not only the language of science but also, as a consequence, the content and form of what is accepted as science (Collins and Pinch 1993; Longino 1990). Such views are encapsulated in the view articulated by Latour and Woolgar (1986), in their seminal study of scientists at work, that:

> science is a form of fiction or discourse like any other, one effect of which is the 'truth effect', which (like all literary effects) arises from textual characteristics, such as the tense of verbs, the structure of enunciation, modalities and so on.
>
> (p. 184)

Likewise, within the science education community, similar debates have taken place between those, such as Tobin and Tippins (1993) and von Glaserfeld (1995) who hold a relativist view of scientific knowledge, seeing it as a social construction unconstrained by the material world, and their critics, for example Matthews (1995) and Osborne (1996), who see it as an objective body of stable and reliable ideas about the world.

The outcome is that, amongst contemporary scholars, the nature of science is seen as a contested domain (Alters 1997; Labinger and Collins 2001; Laudan 1990; Taylor 1996). If the intent of scholarship in the field of history and philosophy of science was to establish a consensual understanding of the foundations of the practice of science then it might be best characterised, as Taylor (1996) has argued, as a 'failed project'. As Stanley and Brickhouse (2001) point out, 'although almost everyone agrees that we ought to teach students about the nature of science, there is considerable disagreement on what version of the nature of science ought to be taught' (p. 47).

In view of this uncertainty, and the lack of any empirical evidence of consensus, the central aim of the first phase of one of the four research projects undertaken by the Evidence-based Practice in Science

Education (EPSE) Research Network (see Appendix, Project 3, for fuller details) was to try to determine empirically the extent of agreement amongst a group of experts consisting of scientists, science communicators, philosophers and sociologists of science, and science educators about those aspects of the nature of science that should be an essential feature of the school science curriculum. In essence, to provide a body of sound and rigorously derived *research evidence* that would *inform* the resolution of this problem for the science education community.

Gathering evidence

The method chosen for eliciting the 'expert' community's view was a three-stage Delphi study. This consists of a set of sequential questionnaires which seek to elicit participants' views and their rationale. None of the participants is aware of the identity of the others. After each questionnaire, the views gathered are summarised and fed back to the participants in the next round. The purpose of this procedure is to provide each participant with an opportunity to reconsider their views in the light of others' arguments, and express again their views and justifications, which may now have changed. This method has been used in other curriculum-based explorations (Doyle 1993; Häussler *et al.* 1980; Smith and Simpson 1995) principally because it minimises the shaping of views by social interaction and hence is a more reliable reflection of the views of the relevant stakeholder community.

The Delphi technique has five advantages felt to be important in gaining the considered opinions of experts:

- It uses group decision-making techniques, involving experts in the field, which have greater validity than those made by an individual or small group of individuals.
- The anonymity of participants and the use of questionnaires avoids the problems commonly associated with group interviews: for example, specious persuasion or 'deference to authority, impact of oral facility, reluctance to modify publicised opinions and bandwagon effects' (Martorella 1991). Moreover, in this case, where participants knowingly held contrary views it reduced the possibility of conflict and enhanced the possibility of a more dispassionate consideration of others' views.
- Consensus reached by the group reflects reasoned opinions, because the Delphi process forces group members to consider logically the problem under study and to provide written responses.

- Commonly, participants are asked to rank the relative significance of any element, as they were in this study, providing data which can be statistically analysed.
- Opinions using the Delphi method can be received from a group of experts who may be geographically separated from one another.

Generally, the minimum number for a Delphi panel is considered to be 10 (Cochran 1983) with reduction in error and improved reliability with increased group size. However, Delbecq et al. (1975) maintain that few new ideas are generated in a homogeneous group once the size exceeds thirty well-chosen participants. For this study, twenty-five experts engaged in the study of science and its communication were recruited.

In this context, we chose to define 'experts' as those with acknowledged expertise in communicating, using or researching the processes and practices of science. Thus we sought views from a sample consisting of five representative individuals from each of the following groups: leading scientists; historians, philosophers and sociologists of science; science educators; those engaged in the public understanding of science or science communication; and primary and secondary teachers of science. In selecting these people we sought to choose a range of people who were known to hold differing opinions and views about science and its nature – that is to make them *broadly representative* of each community. Indeed, two of the individuals participating in this study had been involved in a public meeting where they had differed very strongly. Thus, we deliberately avoided choosing individuals who might be thought likely to agree. Consequently, we feel confident that the choice of the sample was not a major determinant of the outcome.

The criteria used for selecting 'expert' scientists were Fellowship of the Royal Society combined with a requirement that they came from a broad range of the sciences. For the philosophers, sociologists and science educators, it was books and publications of international repute. For science communicators it was a combination of publications of international repute or the holding of an eminent post within the field. In the case of teachers, the notion of 'expert' is not commonly agreed. As the major value of teachers' views was a sense not only of what was important for children to learn, but also what might be pragmatically attainable, we recruited five teachers who had achieved some public recognition for their work, such as individuals who had won national awards for the quality of their teaching or those who were authors of science textbooks in widespread use in the UK.

Of the twenty-five people initially approached by letter, one scientist and one science communicator declined. Two other individuals were recruited to replace them. After the first round, one teacher and one science communicator dropped out, leaving a sample of twenty-three in total. As stated earlier, none of the participants was aware of the identity of the others.

The conduct of the Delphi study and the results

In the first round of the study, opinions were sought about the essential 'ideas about science' that should be taught in the school science curriculum, through the use of an open-ended questionnaire which asked:

1. What, if anything, do you think should be taught about the methods of science?
2. What, if anything, do you think should be taught about the nature of scientific knowledge?
3. What, if anything, do you think should be taught about the institutions and social practices of science?

For each response provided, participants were requested to give as clear a description of each idea as possible, to indicate a particular context in which they thought a person might find the idea useful, and to state *why* such knowledge would be important for an individual to know.

The first round elicited extensive comments from most participants. From these, thirty broad themes were identified and, for each, a summary was composed which attempted to capture the essence of participants' statements and their rationale for its inclusion. The themes were then grouped under three major categories: *The Nature of Scientific Knowledge*, *The Institutions and Social Practices of Science*, and *The Methods of Science*. Figure 2.1 shows a typical summary for one theme 'The Tentative Nature of Scientific Knowledge', and some of the justifications provided by the participants. (For fuller details see the Appendix or Osborne *et al.* 2003.)

Early in the process, we decided to summarise the themes using language of an academic nature that would be understood by most if not all of the participants. Such language has the advantage of offering economy and precision of meaning which is important for communicating ideas clearly and accurately. However, we recognise that, as

---

THE TENTATIVE NATURE OF SCIENTIFIC KNOWLEDGE

Summary
Students should recognise that scientific knowledge is provisional. Current scientific knowledge is the best we have but may be subject to further change given new evidence.

Typical supporting statements
(a)   Scientific knowledge is in a state of continuous change. Theories are the best we can do with the current state of knowledge.
(b)   Theories can be falsified if wrong; they can be modified and extended if correct only in a limited region.
(c)   That scientific knowledge is not fixed for all time because scientific ideas are adapted and revised in the light of new evidence.
(d)   That scientific knowledge is tentative. Scientific knowledge depends on the available evidence and methods for gathering it. As technology makes more precision possible, so new evidence may be revealed, so ideas change. We should always regard scientific knowledge as the best we know at the moment and subject to change.
(e)   They should be taught that scientific knowledge is the best kind of knowledge we have when it comes to understanding the natural world, but this does not make it perfect. They should understand that you have to get by with the best even if it is not perfect and often this will be scientific knowledge.

Figure 2.1   Summary of one theme emerging from Round 1, with typical justifications provided, as presented in Round 2

currently articulated, the ideas embodied in the themes would need to be unpacked and elaborated for a practitioner or general audience.

The process was then repeated by sending the thirty themes, together with representative anonymised comments obtained from individuals in Round 1 (as shown in Figure 2.1). This time, however, participants were requested to rate the importance of each theme to the compulsory school science curriculum on a five-point scale from 1 (no importance) to 5 (very important); to supply some justification for their rating and to respond to the representative supporting statements.

For the third round we reduced the number of themes for consideration by the panel to only the most highly rated themes from Round 2. This decision was taken as there was a concern that 'participant fatigue' might result if the complete set of 'ideas about science' were included, affecting the level of detail in responses towards the end of the questionnaire (Judd 1971). Thus only the themes with a mean rating of greater than 3.6, and/or where more than half the participants rated their importance with a 5, were used for third round – reducing their number in this round to eighteen. In the final round, participants were requested to rate each theme again, based on the premise that it should be *explicitly* taught, to justify their rating, and to comment on ways in which the wording of the summary might be improved to reflect the essence of each 'idea about science'.

Table 2.1 shows the titles of the nine themes for which consensus was achieved in Round 3 with their headings, the summary statements used in Round 3 to encapsulate their meaning using key phrases articulated by the Delphi panel, and the mean ratings (and standard deviations) in Rounds 2 and 3.

Rationale for each theme

Participants were urged to provide detailed comments in Round 3 to justify and explain the rating given for each theme based on the premise that it should be *explicitly* taught. A summary of these comments for one theme is shown in Figure 2.2. Such comments are an essential component to the aim and purpose of this study. For without these remarks, the Delphi study, whilst successfully establishing what 'experts' believed should be taught, would have lacked any rationale which answered the more fundamental question of *why* such elements should be taught.

A sample of the kind of the warrants provided by participants is reflected in their comments about the theme 'Scientific Methods and Critical Testing'. Individuals argued that this theme is the 'core process on which the whole edifice of science is built'. The experimental method was said to be 'what defines science', and was the 'central thrust of scientific research' and as such must be an essential part of the school science curriculum. One participant stated that students frequently formed the view that the purpose of practical work was to teach them techniques; and that 'they do not understand that, in the research world of science, careful experimentation is used to test hypotheses'.

Table 2.1 Final set of nine themes for which consensus emerged from the Delphi study, with ratings in Round 2

Theme title and summary	Round 2		Round 3	
	Mean	S.D.	Mean	S.D.
NATURE OF SCIENTIFIC KNOWLEDGE				
Science and Certainty (Round 3) / Tentative nature of scientific knowledge (Round 2) Students should appreciate why much scientific knowledge, particularly that taught in school science, is well-established and beyond reasonable doubt, and why other scientific knowledge is more open to legitimate doubt. It should be explained that current scientific knowledge is the best we have but may be subject to change in the future, given new evidence or new interpretations of old evidence.	4.3	0.96	4.2	0.93
Historical development of scientific knowledge Students should be taught some of the historical background to the development of scientific knowledge.	4.0	0.95	4.3	0.94
METHODS OF SCIENCE				
Scientific methods and critical testing (Round 3) / Experimental methods and critical testing (Round 2) Students should be taught that science uses the experimental method to test ideas, and, in particular, about certain basic techniques such as the use of controls. It should be made clear that the outcome of a single experiment is rarely sufficient to establish a knowledge claim.	4.4	0.73	4.4	0.79
Analysis and interpretation of data Students should be taught that the practice of science involves skilful analysis and interpretation of data. Scientific knowledge claims do not emerge simply from the data but through a process of interpretation and theory building that can require sophisticated skills. It is possible for scientists legitimately to come to different interpretations of the same data, and therefore, to disagree.	4.1	1.27	4.2	0.88

Theme title and summary	Round 2		Round 3	
	Mean	S.D.	Mean	S.D.
Hypothesis and prediction Students should be taught that scientists develop hypotheses and predictions about natural phenomena. This process is essential to the development of new knowledge claims.	4.0	1.07	4.2	1.00
Diversity of scientific thinking (Round 3) / Diversity of scientific method (Round 2) Students should be taught that science uses a range of methods and approaches and that there is no one scientific method or approach.	4.0	1.07	4.2	0.71
Creativity Students should appreciate that science is an activity that involves creativity and imagination as much as many other human activities, and that some scientific ideas are enormous intellectual achievements. Scientists, as much as any other profession, are passionate and involved humans whose work relies on inspiration and imagination.	4.0	1.13	4.4	0.72
Science and questioning Students should be taught that an important aspect of the work of a scientist is the continual and cyclical process of asking questions and seeking answers, which then lead to new questions. This process leads to the emergence of new scientific theories and techniques which are then tested empirically.	4.0	1.28	4.2	0.68

INSTITUTIONS AND SOCIAL PRACTICES IN SCIENCE

Cooperation and collaboration in development of scientific knowledge Students should be taught that scientific work is a communal and competitive activity. Whilst individuals may make significant contributions, scientific work is often carried out in groups, frequently of a multidisciplinary and international nature. New knowledge claims are generally shared and, to be accepted by the community, must survive a process of critical peer review.	3.6	1.47	4.2	0.79

SCIENTIFIC METHOD AND CRITICAL TESTING

Participants viewed the theme as the articulation of the 'core process on which the whole edifice of science is built'. The experimental method was said to be 'what defines science', and was the 'central thrust of scientific research' and as such must be an essential part of the school science curriculum. One participant stated that students frequently formed the view that the purpose of practical work was to teach them techniques; 'they do not understand that in the research world of science, careful experimentation is used to test hypotheses'. The theme was seen to provide opportunities to develop what was already a major component of the English national curriculum for science and to highlight the importance of testing ideas as the basis of science. The testing of ideas was an important issue for one participant who expressed the view that many science courses and texts labelled as 'experiments' what were in reality 'demonstrations' and therefore not a test of scientific ideas.

Figure 2.2   Summary of participants' views on one theme, based on Round 3 responses

Whilst some of the above points are perhaps to be expected given its centrality for science, arguments for themes that are not a central aspect of the existing curriculum were equally strong. For instance, the importance of the theme 'Diversity of Scientific Thinking' was its 'potential to provide students with first-hand experience of the breadth of scientific activity and that it would 'help nip scientism in the bud', indicating to pupils that the world might be explored through a range of means. The theme offered opportunities to develop an understanding that 'science is not rigid – a number of methods may be used to solve the same problem' and encouraged teachers to 'get away from the simplistic notions of how science is done'. In short, it would help counter the pervasive lay notion that science is conducted using a singular method which leads to unequivocal answers.

Consensus and stability

The issue here is: what level of agreement constitutes consensus? There is little guidance in the literature to inform such decisions. Hence, it was necessary for us to decide on an appropriate figure. For this Delphi study, it was defined as a minimum of two-thirds of participants rating a theme as 4 or above on the 1–5 scale. Stability was defined as a shift of one-third or less in participants' ratings between Rounds 2 and 3.

The ratings for the theme 'Cooperation and Collaboration' were somewhat less stable than the others across Rounds 2 and 3. The final theme was a product of merging two themes from Round 2 – 'Science as a Human, Collaborative Activity' and 'Cooperation and Collaboration'. This substantive change may have been the cause of the significant difference in its rating between the two rounds.

Conclusions

The findings of this study provide empirical evidence that there *is* a high level of agreement around certain features of a basic knowledge and understanding *about* science (Table 2.1) – aspects which are seen as both significant and essential. In addition, the low variation in rankings suggests that these features are uncontroversial both within, and across, the relevant academic communities. Given that the 'experts' chosen to participate in this study were deliberately selected to represent the divergence of views in the stakeholder communities, we would argue that the findings of this study suggest that, beneath the public disagreements about the nature of science, there is considerable agreement, in broad terms, about the 'ideas about science' which should be an essential element of the school science curriculum.

Nevertheless, it is important to recognise that the findings of this study represent participants' ranking of importance of the themes rather than a definitive judgement about what should or should not be included. The nine themes represent the *basic minimum* that any simplified account of science should incorporate. Were we to use a less demanding criterion for consensus – for instance, that a simple majority of the participants agreed that any theme was important or very important – then the following themes would also be included:

- Science and technology (65 per cent)
- Moral and ethical dimensions in the development of scientific knowledge (61 per cent)

- The empirical base of scientific knowledge (61 per cent)
- Cumulative and revisionary nature of scientific knowledge (61 per cent)
- Observation and measurement (56 per cent)
- The characteristics of scientific knowledge (52 per cent)
- Specific methods of science (52 per cent)

Hence, what the results of the study show are those elements which are considered to be most important – that is, a set of core elements essential to any simplified account of the nature of science suitable for the school science curriculum. Whilst we are conscious that the level of agreement might diminish if the statements were unpacked in more detail, any disagreements would be just that – matters of detail rather than about the central idea embodied in any theme.

Many of the participants recognised that the account of science represented by these themes is limited, and that it is difficult to specify clearly and unambiguously the key 'ideas about science' that students should grasp. Indeed, from our analysis of the participants' comments, it is clear that many felt that some of the ideas were intertwined and not resolvable into separate propositions. In essence, it was the research process that required the separation and resolution of these components in order to weight their significance and import. There is no suggestion, however, that they should be communicated and represented in that manner in the curriculum.

What the study clearly does not do is to say anything about how those ideas might be taught or assessed. That was not its intent. In addition, the majority of the members of this group lack the relevant expertise to advise on their implementation. Nevertheless, for teaching purposes (see Chapter 7), such themes do need expanding and translating for teachers. Thus, they would need rewriting in a less academic language and they would need exemplification to help communicate their meaning to teachers and others. Such a task is invariably subjective and interpretive, requiring the ideas to be expanded and explained, but at least in this case, it would have a sound empirical foundation.

Discussion and implications

The essential function of research of this kind is to improve the quality of information and argument that informs the decision-making process about curricula. This study contributes in two ways: (a) by showing that there is expert agreement; and (b) by providing an extensive rationale for the themes and their incorporation. Any curriculum developed on the basis of such evidence can therefore be claimed to be research evidence-informed. Without such evidence, the specification of curriculum objectives becomes reliant on the subjective viewpoints of key individuals and/or the rhetorical force with which these are presented.

For instance, the current version of the English national curriculum for science (DfEE/QCA 1999) provides some recognition of the significance that should be given to 'ideas and evidence in science' with an eponymous component. Comparing this curriculum to the results of this study, it is possible to see elements of most of the major nine themes. It might, therefore, be reasonable to think that the treatment of the nature of science is satisfactory. There is, however, no treatment of one of the major themes from the Delphi study, 'The Diversity of Scientific Thinking'. Few science curricula anywhere have recognised a fundamental division in the sciences that Gould (1991), Rudolph (2000) and Frodeman (2003) make between historical reconstruction and empirical testing. In the former, in sciences such as geology and palaeontology, as Rudolph (2000) argues, 'the immediate goal . . . is not the development of a model, but rather the establishment of reliable record of what has occurred and when' (p. 410). Also no curriculum of which we are aware has taken the step of introducing, as a valid scientific approach, the atheoretical search for patterns in data – the basis of epidemiology – which is helpful in distinguishing causal from correlational relationships. Rather, school science remains dominated by the empirical and exact sciences of physics and chemistry and their hypothetico-deductive methods.

Thus, the Delphi study provides a body of evidence with which it is possible to mount a critique of the extant curriculum and to inform contemporary thinking of its development and transformation. Why, for instance, is there a minimalist treatment of geology and plate tectonics – the study of which shows clearly how scientists can initially misinterpret or reject data strongly suggesting that the continents were at one time connected? This aspect falls under the theme 'Analysis and Interpretation of Data' – but also illustrates and exposes 'The Diversity of Scientific Thinking'.

The evidence provided by research of this nature does, however, have its limitations. It does not answer the teacher's question of how these statements might be operationalised into teaching strategies, or what kinds of activities and materials might be needed to support their teaching. So this evidence is not a contribution to research evidence-based practice. Nor can it inform any answer to the question of whether these themes should be taught explicitly or should implicitly permeate all science lessons – an issue which was raised by some Delphi participants. First attempts to incorporate some of these ideas in new English courses, such as the AS-level *Science for Public Understanding* (Millar and Hunt 2002) or the pilot scheme *Twenty First Century Science* (21st Century Science team 2003), have chosen to address 'ideas about science' through specific topics such as 'Air Pollution', 'Keeping Healthy' or 'Earth in the Universe', which may raise issues, for instance, from two of the themes emerging from this study – 'Analysis and Inter- pretation of Data' and 'The Tentative Nature of Scientific Knowledge'. Nevertheless, some of the themes of this Delphi study, such as 'Creativity', pose significant pedagogical challenges and may simply be beyond what school science is capable of offering its students.

The function of studies such as this is to do two things. The first is to see if there is any level of agreement about what should be taught in the stakeholder communities. The normal means of determining curriculum content is to consult 'the great and the good' and then to rely on a small group of individuals to distil what they have said in a not very rigorous manner. Such a process risks giving too much emphasis to one group, does not weight individuals' views equally, and is too reliant on subjective interpretation. The second achievement of such studies is that they not only clarify what should be taught but also provide an explicit rationale for its inclusion. The outcome is that curriculum specification is more likely to be a practice that is research-evidence informed and that teachers will have an explicit justification for what society asks them to teach. In short, curriculum specification will have become more of a science and less of an art.

Summary

A Delphi study, involving three rounds of questionnaires, with a panel of 25 representatives of five key groups of 'stakeholders' in the science curriculum, showed a high level of agreement about broad curriculum objectives as regards teaching students about the nature of science. Nine themes were identified which the majority of the panel endorsed as important learning objectives for all students by age 16. There was little evidence of significant differences of opinion or priority among the groups who made up the panel. Whilst differences may well emerge when this is taken to the level of detail required to design teaching activities and assessment tasks, this shows how research can play a valuable role in establishing the consistency of views of different interest groups, and helping to build a more explicit consensus about curriculum objectives and priorities.

Chapter 3

Using research to clarify learning goals and measure outcomes

Whereas ideas about the nature of science (the subject of Chapter 2) have been much disputed and argued over by philosophers, historians and sociologists of science, there is little or no disagreement among scientists about the scientific concepts and ideas that are taught at school level. There may be disputes about scientific knowledge at the 'frontiers', but the core ideas are established beyond reasonable doubt. There is also considerable agreement amongst science educators about the parts of the scientific canon that should be taught at school level. The same science topics feature on school science curricula the world over. There is also considerable stability over time: in England, for example, whilst there have been frequent minor modifications to the content of the science curriculum over the years, most of the core topics in the science national curriculum – Newtonian mechanics, electric circuits, atomic/molecular models of chemical reactions, photosynthesis and respiration, and so on – were taught fifty, even a hundred, years ago. This consensus about what we should teach in school science may, however, be rather less solid than it initially seems, if we look at the curriculum in more detail – and in particular at the *intended learning outcomes*.

Learning outcomes

When we teach students about forces and motion (to take an example), what exactly do we want them to learn and, perhaps more importantly,

Authored by Robin Millar and Vicky Hames

to be able to do as a result? The curriculum may include a list of detailed learning objectives, but the clearest pointer to the outcomes that are most valued is the form of assessment used to judge students' performance. And this reveals a tension. Although the rhetoric of school science commonly endorses 'teaching for understanding' as the most important aim, assessment practices often emphasise recall of facts, rules and conventions – rather than understanding of fundamental ideas, concepts, models and theories. In England, for example, the national assessments of students' performance in science at ages 11, 14 and 16 have been criticised on these grounds (Osborne and Ratcliffe 2001; Brooks 2002). As in many countries, the tests used are 'broad brush' measures of performance in science as a whole, often emphasising those aspects of science learning which are easiest to assess. There is, of course, a practical reason for including questions testing recall of knowledge of specific facts and conventions: these are more accessible to lower-achieving students, who might struggle with probes of understanding, and so enable more students to demonstrate some attainment.

Research on science learning, on the other hand, has tended to focus on students' understanding of fundamental ideas, concepts and models in specific science domains, exploring and documenting the ways in which students try to explain common everyday phenomena, how they construe taught ideas, and common patterns of reasoning. A large body of research, carried out in many countries and with students of a wide range of ages, has documented these ideas and patterns in considerable detail. The bibliography developed by Pfundt and Duit, listing around 7000 sources in its most recent edition (Duit 2006), gives an indication of the scale of this research effort. Several of these studies have shown that many students who obtain satisfactory or good scores on typical end-of-course assessment tests are unable to give correct answers to probes of understanding of basic ideas and concepts (Mazur 1997; Redish 2003). The two kinds of assessment instrument are measuring different things.

Researchers – and the rhetoric of science education – have tended to value an understanding of fundamental ideas more than the ability to recall facts and conventions, as this seems a more important, more valuable, and potentially more durable, outcome of science education. Also, coming to an understanding of important and powerful ideas, even in a simplified form, is likely to be more satisfying for learners than trying to commit to memory a large number of unconnected facts and conventions. And an emphasis on ideas, and on how we have arrived at them, enables science to be taught in a manner which is more faithful to its underlying epistemology.

Assessment, then, is important, not only as a means of monitoring individual students' progress in learning, but also as a way of making clear the learning goals. The role of assessment in clarifying learning outcomes is particularly critical if our aim is to improve students' understanding. We often talk of 'teaching for understanding'; but what do we mean when we claim that someone 'understands' or 'does not understand' something? 'Understanding' cannot be directly observed; it can only be inferred from an observed performance of some kind. In science teaching, the kinds of performances we take to be indicators of understanding are the things students write or say, or in some cases their actions in response to certain stimuli (questions or tasks). The ability to answer a question, or set of questions, about topic X then provides an 'operational definition' of 'understanding of X', and perhaps also a means of measuring it on a scale that enables us to identify change and improvement. We might, of course, want to debate how good an indicator, or measure, of understanding of a topic any particular question or set of questions is, and whether the ability to respond appropriately to questions of a particular type reflects the kind of understanding we value. But the great value of having an operational definition of 'understanding of X' is that it greatly clarifies the intended learning outcomes, and puts these 'on the table', open to scrutiny and debate.

A means of measuring learning outcomes is also critical for the idea of research evidence-based practice. This depends (see Figure 1.2) on collecting evidence that shows the extent to which a teaching intervention achieves its intended outcomes, perhaps by comparing it with another intervention, or with the range of interventions that constitute current 'normal' practice. If these outcomes include 'understanding', then we should acknowledge that there are no standardised or widely accepted measures of 'understanding' of any of the major topics or ideas in the sciences, comparable, for instance, to those used to measure reading ability. We suspect that the same may be true of many other curriculum subjects. The remainder of this chapter explores what might be involved in developing such measures.

Developing research evidence-informed assessment tools

The aim of EPSE Project 1 (see Appendix) was to explore the impact on science teachers' practices of providing them with large banks of diagnostic questions for several science domains, in a form that they could readily use in their own teaching. By a 'diagnostic question', we mean one that probes students' understanding of a specific point or issue, where students' responses give reasonably clear evidence that they have grasped the scientific view or that they hold a common 'alternative' one. Diagnostic questions may also give some insights into the reasoning underlying correct and incorrect answers. Questions of this sort might be used for both formative and summative assessment purposes. The questions were based on the kinds of probes devised by researchers to elicit learners' understanding of fundamental ideas and concepts in these domains. Our hypothesis was that the question banks would direct teachers' attention towards key ideas known to pose learning difficulties, and would make it easier for them to monitor their students' ideas and understandings before and during the teaching of a topic – and that this might stimulate them to modify their teaching in various ways.

The question banks were developed in close collaboration with a small group of practitioners. This group identified the science domains for which diagnostic questions would be most useful, on the basis of their experience. The questions and interview probes previously used by researchers provided a starting point. These were collected, and scrutinised in detail by the group, often leading to changes to improve the clarity of text or diagrams, and to convert them to formats that could be more quickly and easily used in classrooms. A critical design criterion for teachers was that questions should yield data, on all the students in a class, that could be quickly assimilated and so could influence subsequent teaching decisions. As part of the development process, questions were pilot tested, followed by interviews with samples of pupils to explore their ideas further and check how well their written responses reflected their understandings. Several examples of questions developed are shown later in this chapter.

These diagnostic question banks, then, are strongly and explicitly informed by research. The questions focus on understanding of ideas that research has identified as posing significant learning difficulties for many students. As well as providing evidence of the accepted understanding, many are also designed to reveal misconceptions, or 'alternative' ways of explaining and reasoning about phenomena, that research has shown to be common. Research on learning has also stimulated and informed the detailed analysis of subject matter needed to organise and present them in an order which suggests a learning pathway through the domain.

Creating research evidence-informed teaching tools of this sort is not a trivial task. Devising each question involves making concrete and precise one aspect of what we mean by 'understanding' of the idea that it is probing. Using research to inform teaching is not simply a matter of 'implementing' insights and findings from research, but involves *creating a new artefact* which embodies these in a readily useable form. This, as we have discussed above, leads to considerable clarification of learning objectives. It also makes it very much easier to communicate these objectives. In place of tacit assumptions about expected learning, the questions make clear and explicit the sorts of tasks we expect students to be able to accomplish if they have learned what we wanted them to learn. Hence they facilitate the kind of precise and focused dialogue about teaching and learning that is essential to the development of practice, and which can help to make practice more consistent.

Promoting research evidence-informed practice

How then, might these banks of diagnostic questions promote more research evidence-informed practice? We see two main ways:

- They may encourage teachers to spend more class time on ideas that are known from research to be challenging but are also particularly important for the development of understanding (by drawing attention to them and by suggesting activities that might help to change them).
- They make it easier for teachers to collect high-quality evidence of their own students' learning, during the teaching process. So teachers' decisions can be based on better evidence, which they themselves have collected, of their own students' current under- standings.

If the second of these is carried out systematically, so that the evidence collected could be displayed, and this evidence is then used to test the effectiveness of specific interventions, these might also become examples of research evidence-based practice, as we have characterised it in Chapter 1 (in Figure 1.2). These issues will be explored further in Chapter 6, where we discuss a set of case studies exploring how a group of teachers, provided with one of these diagnostic question banks, used it in their own practice, and the effects this had.

For the remainder of this chapter, however, we want to present some findings that arose from the development of these question banks, which highlight an issue of central importance to the development of research evidence-based practice – the nature and the quality of the instruments we use to measure learning outcomes.

Measuring 'understanding'

We have already made the point that 'understanding' cannot be observed or measured directly. It then becomes important to ask how good any given question or task, or set of questions or tasks, is for indicating understanding or detecting a specific misunderstanding. One way to explore this is to look at the consistency of individual students' answers to several questions probing understanding of the same idea, such as those shown in Figures 3.1 and 3.2.

These are examples of two-tier questions, with the first tier asking the student to identify a specific prediction and the second asking them to indicate the best explanation for their choice (Treagust 1988). As well as moving the focus away from recall and towards understanding, this question format helps to detect students who are guessing (and so choose a pair of answer options that are inconsistent). Both questions probe understanding of the same science idea – that electric current is the same size at all points around a simple (series) circuit. This is counter-intuitive for many students, who reason that some (or all) of the current must be used up in components, such as light bulbs, that the current flows through. In Question 1 (Figure 3.1), someone who understands the *scientific model* of electric current would choose option 3 for part (a) followed by option 1 for part (b). On the other hand, someone who thinks of current as flowing from the positive battery terminal round to the negative battery terminal (anti-clockwise), and believes that some is used up by the bulb, would choose option 1 for part (a) followed by option 2 for part (b). If they think of current as flowing in the *other* direction (clockwise), they would chose option 2 followed by option 2. We might label this model of electric current an *attenuation model* – the current is thought to be attenuated by each component it passes through. A third group of students may think that the bulb uses up *all* of the current – a *consumption model* of electric current. They would answer option 1 followed by option 3, or option 2 followed by option 3, depending on which direction they thought the current went round. In interpreting students' responses, of course, we are reasoning in the opposite direction – hypothesising the student's

Q1

In this circuit, a battery is connected to a bulb. The bulb is lit.

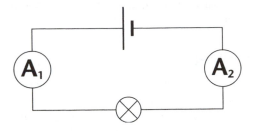

(a) What can you say about the readings on the two ammeters?

Tick ONE box (✓)

☐   The reading on ammeter A_1 is bigger.

☐   The reading on ammeter A_2 is bigger.

☐   The readings on the two ammeters are the same.

(b) How would you explain this?

Tick ONE box (✓)

☐   The electric current is the same all round the circuit.

☐   **Some** of the electric current is used up by the bulb.

☐   **All** of the electric current is used up by the bulb.

Figure 3.1   Question 1: Electric current on either side of a bulb

underlying model of electric current from the answer pattern they provide. The patterns of answers to Question 2 (Figure 3.2) can be similarly interpreted in terms of the same models.

Answers to these two questions were collected from a sample of 210 14-year-old students from five secondary schools in England. Projected national test grades for each student indicated that this sample was somewhat above the national average in science performance. As our interest here is in comparing a student's responses to two or more questions testing understanding of the same idea, and not on their overall level of performance, this positive bias in the sample is not important. The students' answers were analysed as we have described above – using the pattern of responses to the two parts of the question

Q2

In this circuit, a battery is connected to a resistor R and an ammeter. The ammeter reads 0.2 amps.

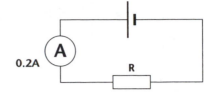

0.2A

The ammeter is then moved to the other side of the circuit.

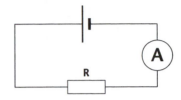

(a) What is the reading on the ammeter now?

Tick ONE box (✓)

☐ More than 0.2 amps.

☐ Exactly 0.2 amps.

☐ Less then 0.2 amps, but not zero.

☐ Zero.

(b) How would you explain this?

Tick ONE box (✓)

☐ The current is the same all round the circuit.

☐ **Some** of the current is used up by the resistor.

☐ **All** of the current is used up by the resistor.

Figure 3.2 Question 2: Moving an ammeter to the other side of a circuit

to identify the model of electric current consistent with their answer pattern. The results are summarised in Table 3.1.

First, it is worth noting that almost all students gave an answer consistent with one of these models, 197 (94 per cent) and 199 students (95 per cent) respectively. This strongly suggests that answers are based on reasoning rather than guesswork. Only 128 (61 per cent), however,

Table 3.1 Number of 14-year-old students' answers consistent with each model of current in Questions Q1 and Q2

	Answers to Q2					
	scientific model	attenuation (CC)	attenuation (EF)	consumption (CC)	other responses	Total
Answers to Q1 scientific model	65	31	15	1	3	115
attenuation (CC)	4	38	4		2	48
attenuation (EF)	7	11	10		2	30
consumption (CC)		1	1		1	3
consumption (EF)		1	1			1
other responses	6	3	1		3	13
Total	82	85	31	1	11	210

(Key: CC = conventional current direction; EF = electron flow direction) gave answers consistent with the *same* model to *both* questions. Of these, 31 per cent (65 students) answered in line with the scientific model, and 30 per cent (63 students) the attenuation model (though only 48 (23 per cent) used *the same* current direction each time). The data show how misleading it would be to take either question on its own as an indicator that a student understood the idea of electric current. Of the 115 students who answered Q1 in line with the scientific model, only 65 gave answers to Q2 that were consistent with this model. Of the 82 students who answered Q2 in line with the scientific model, only 65 did so when answering Q1.

A possible explanation for the difference in response patterns to Questions 1 and 2 is that students think of a bulb as behaving differently from a resistor. So we explored this further by collecting responses from a further sample of 169 15-year-old students, again drawn from five schools, to a test containing Q1 and another which was *exactly* the same apart from having a resistor in place of the bulb. The pattern of responses was similar. Most were consistent with either the scientific or attenuation model – but again there was considerable inconsistency in many students' use of these two models in answering the two questions. Again, either question alone would give a rather inaccurate measure of 'understanding' of electric current in a series circuit.

The same kind of inconsistency in answers to questions was also apparent in other topic areas. In another study, we collected data on students' understanding of forces and motion, from 197 14-year-old students, drawn from five schools. Other data collected suggested that the average science performance of this sample was also somewhat above the national average. These students were given a set of questions on forces and motion that included those shown in Figures 3.3 and 3.4. The counter-intuitive idea at the heart of the Newtonian explanation of motion is that a force is needed only to *change* motion (increase or decrease speed, or change direction) but not to *maintain* motion. So the resultant force (that is, the total force taking account of the directions of individual forces) on any object moving at a steady speed is zero. And, in the case of an object which has been set in motion (for example, by being pushed or kicked or thrown) and is now slowing down, the resultant force is not in the direction of motion but in the opposite direction. Many students, however, have 'alternative' views about the relationship between forces and motion, associating force with velocity rather than with *change* in velocity. So they reason that there must be a force on a moving object in the direction in which it is going – and perhaps even that the resultant force must be in that direction.

Q3

A spacecraft is drifting through space. It is very far away from all other objects. There is no air in space, so there is no air resistance. The spacecraft is moving in a straight line at a constant speed.

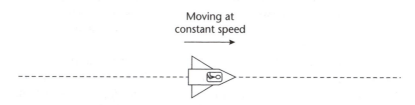

Moving at
constant speed

What force must the rockets exert on the spacecraft to keep it moving in this direction at constant speed?

Tick ONE box (✓)

☐ No force is needed.

☐ A constant force towards the right.

☐ A steadily increasing force towards the right.

Figure 3.3 Question 3: Force needed to keep a spacecraft moving

In Q3, answer option 1 is in agreement with the Newtonian model, whereas option 2 is in line with a force–velocity model, that is, with reasoning that associates force directly with velocity. (The third option was included with the next part of the question in mind, where students were asked about the force required to make the spacecraft speed up steadily.) In Q4, answer option 3 is in line with the Newtonian model, whereas options 1 and 2 suggest reasoning that associates force directly with velocity. (The fourth option is offered for completeness, rather than to detect any specific known misconception.) Table 3.2 shows the pattern of 14-year-old students' responses. Almost all chose the options that correspond either to the Newtonian understanding or to the common force–velocity association. The consistency of students' answers, however, is rather low, with 100 giving answers in line with the same model both times, and 90 giving answers in line with different models.

Q4

A car is travelling along a level road. Two forces acting on it are:

- a **driving force** caused by the engine.
- a **counter force** caused by friction and air resistance.

The car is travelling at a steady speed. How do the driving force and counter force compare?

Tick ONE box (✓)

☐ The driving force is **quite a lot bigger** than the counter force.

☐ The driving force is **a little bit bigger** than the counter force.

☐ The driving force is **equal to** the counter force.

☐ The driving force is **smaller than** the counter force.

Figure 3.4 Question 4: Driving force and counter force when a car is moving at a steady speed

The same questions were also included in a set answered by a sample of 250 16-year-old students, drawn from six schools. A significantly higher proportion (than of the 14-year-olds) chose the answer consistent with the Newtonian model for each question, though this was still only 66 per cent of the sample for Q3 and 52 per cent for Q4 (Table 3.3). The increase in the proportion answering *both* questions in line with the Newtonian model was larger than this: 91 out of 250 (36 per cent) compared with 39 out of 197 (20 per cent). On the other hand, 111 students (44 per cent of the sample) gave an answer in line with the Newtonian model for one of the questions, and an answer in line with the force–velocity model for the other. So whilst the overall pattern of answers does show some movement towards the Newtonian model, there is still much evidence of uncertainty about models – and either

Table 3.2   Number of 14-year-old students' answers consistent with each model of the force–motion relationship in Questions Q3 and Q4

		Answers to Q4			
		scientific model	*force–velocity model*	*other responses*	**Total**
Answers to Q3	scientific model	39	35	1	75
	force–velocity model	55	61		116
	other responses	3	3		6
	Total	97	99	1	197

Table 3.3   Number of 16-year-old students' answers consistent with each model of the force–motion relationship in Questions Q3 and Q4

		Answers to Q4			
		scientific model	*force–velocity model*	*other responses*	**Total**
Answers to Q3	scientific model	91	37	1	129
	force–velocity model	74	47		121
	Total	165	84	1	250

question alone would provide poor evidence of 'understanding' of the relationship between force and motion in the Newtonian model.

Some implications for research evidence-based practice

What, then, might we conclude from all of this? First we should make clear that the data presented above are only a very small fraction of those we collected on 11-, 14- and 16-year-old students' understanding of key ideas in several science topic areas. Many other similar examples could have been presented of inconsistency in students' answers to two or more questions probing understanding of the same idea. Second, similar findings have been reported by researchers working on other science topics (Engel Clough and Driver 1986; Finegold and Gorsky 1991; Palmer 1998). In the context of this book, our principal interest is in the implications of this for research evidence-based practice. For this, valid and reliable measures of intended learning outcomes are a prerequisite. Without them, even the most rigorous research design cannot provide clear or useful evidence. For example, to move towards evidence-based teaching of simple electric circuit theory would involve evaluating the outcomes of one or more interventions. But which outcomes do we want, and how do we measure them? If 'understanding' of electric circuits is our aim, we want to show that teaching electric circuits using intervention A leads to better understanding than intervention B. In practice, all we can do is show that intervention A leads to higher scores *on the particular test we have used*. So it is critically important to establish that this test is an adequate measure of 'understanding' of electric circuits (or of those specific ideas about electric circuits that we are teaching).

Our findings suggest that the development of a measure of 'understanding', even of a relatively clear and well-defined idea, is far from trivial. It involves pre-testing of questions to check that students interpret them as we intend, and that we correctly interpret their answers. Any test made up from such questions should then be evaluated by a panel of 'experts' (teachers and others) to judge its *face validity*, that is, that it appears to measure the things it is said to measure, so that we can reasonably assert that any student scoring well on it 'understands' the idea it is testing. It is also useful to check that all the questions contribute to a measure of the same underlying construct. There are various standard ways of doing this. One is to look at correlations between students' scores on each question and their total scores on the whole test, to identify and perhaps remove any questions that produce strange response patterns. Commonly used parameters such as Cronbach's alpha and KR-20 (Satterly 1981) also provide a useful check on the reliability of a test, but do not identify specific 'problem' questions. Another approach is to assess whether a set of questions appears to form a unidimensional scale, by exploring how well the pattern of student responses fits a Rasch model (Bond and Fox 2001) or a more complex item-response theory (IRT) model (Sadler 1998). When this has all been done, there are still decisions to be taken about how many questions on each point or idea are needed, and what score will be taken as indicating 'understanding'. We do not want to imply that this is impossible – just that it is demanding, and that it has not yet been done for any of the main science domains or key ideas.

Sound outcome measures are a prerequisite for any evaluation of an educational intervention. But their importance is even more critical for research designs that claim to be able to provide a strong warrant for causal claims, such as randomised controlled trials. The soundness of conclusions that can be drawn from evaluation studies depends at least as much on the quality of the instruments used, as on the research design; even the most sophisticated designs are undermined if the outcome measures used are unconvincing.

If educational outcomes were placed on a scale from 'relatively easy to measure' to 'relatively difficult to measure', 'understanding the scientific model of electric current' would surely be towards the 'relatively easy' end of the scale. The data presented above, however, suggest that it poses a considerable challenge nonetheless. If we want to make educational practice in science (or in any curriculum subject) more evidence-based, we need to put much more effort than at present into the development of thoroughly pre-tested and consensually agreed measures of the learning outcomes we are most concerned about.

Returning to the issues with which we began this chapter, we would suggest that trying harder to do so would bring a major benefit – by obliging us to make much more clear and precise what our learning objectives really are, by operationalising these in terms of observable performances by students – that is, by stating clearly what students who have achieved the intended outcome can *do*, which those who have not cannot. This level of clarity about learning objectives is valuable, whether or not it is used to compare the effectiveness of different teaching approaches to the same topic. In the areas in which we have worked, we have made some progress towards such instruments, but have also shown that there is still a considerable way to go.

Summary

Assessment tasks provide us with the clearest indication of the learning outcomes of a curriculum. They have a particularly important role in clarifying the desired outcomes when our aim is to improve students' 'understanding'. Comparing students' responses to pairs of diagnostic questions probing understanding of the same idea, however, showed that inconsistent answers were relatively common – suggesting that many students focus on surface details of the question rather than the underlying principle. So several such questions are needed to give a reliable indication of a student's understanding. This highlights the difficulty we face in measuring the outcomes of educational interventions, to evaluate or compare their effectiveness.

Chapter 4

Designing research evidence-informed teaching interventions

In Chapters 2 and 3, we have considered how the process of specifying broad curriculum aims, and identifying whether those aims have been achieved, might be informed by research evidence. This chapter describes a research evidence-informed approach to specifying detailed learning aims and designing teaching interventions. In Chapter 5, we will go on to report on the evaluation of these designed teaching interventions, and consider whether future instances of teaching using them could reasonably be regarded as research evidence-based practice.

The problem

The literature on students' learning of scientific concepts is extensive (see, for example, the bibliography of research studies compiled by Duit 2006). Significant theoretical influences on this body of research include Jean Piaget's genetic epistemology and David Ausubel's cognitive psychology. In 1968, Ausubel wrote, 'The most important single factor influencing learning is what the learner already knows, ascertain this and teach him accordingly' (p. vi). Literally thousands of empirical studies exist which inform science educators about *what the learner already knows*. However, relatively little work has been carried out to clarify what might be involved in *teaching accordingly*, and the impact of this research on the practices of day-to-day science teaching has not been great (Duit and Treagust 1998).

Furthermore, some are sceptical as to whether teaching based on information about students' existing knowledge leads to gains in

Authored by Phil Scott, John Leach, Andy Hind and Jenny Lewis

students' understanding (for example, Matthews 1997). Although there are a few studies in the literature that do provide evidence of improvements in student learning against specified goals, following research evidence-informed teaching interventions (for example, Brown and Clement 1991; Tiberghien 2000; Viennot and Rainson 1999), such studies generally do not consider the role of the *teacher* in implementing the teaching. Often, the teachers in these studies have worked very closely, over an extended period of time, with the research team. There is little, or no, evidence that teachers less closely involved with the research process can replicate any improvements observed in student learning.

In this chapter we describe how research on teaching and learning science was used to inform the design of three teaching interventions. The interventions were aimed at secondary school students. The first two present introductory ideas about plant nutrition and the behaviour of simple electrical circuits. The third intervention provides opportunities for students to revise how physical and chemical change processes are modelled and explained in terms of the behaviour of particles.

In designing the teaching interventions, we drew upon two fundamentally different groups of insights from research. The first group includes findings from empirical research studies, which are commonly referred to as 'evidence'. By contrast, the second group of insights are theoretical, and include insights into the nature of knowledge, thinking, learning and teaching. These insights have been developed through research and scholarship in science education and other fields, and are typically referred to as 'theory' rather than 'evidence'. Nonetheless, however, they influence how findings from empirical studies are interpreted and used as *evidence* about something. We refer to such insights about the nature of knowledge, thinking, learning and teaching as our *theoretical framing perspective*.

This chapter describes the multiple influences on the design of the three teaching interventions – evidence about teaching and learning specific science content (interpreted through our theoretical framing perspective), other insights about teaching and learning science that come from our theoretical framing perspective, and insights about teaching that come from professional practice. We conclude by discussing the extent to which the teaching interventions could reasonably be claimed to be research evidence-informed, making a case for the development of *worked examples* which embody insights from research for the purpose of improving practice.

Theoretical framing perspective

A social constructivist perspective is fundamental to our thinking about teaching and learning science (Leach and Scott 2002). This perspective draws upon empirical studies of science learners' characteristic ways of thinking and talking about the natural world, and Vygotsky's account of how individuals come to understand disciplinary knowledge, such as the natural sciences.

According to Vygotsky, the learning of disciplinary knowledge involves a passage from social to individual planes (Vygotsky 1978). In the first instance, language and other semiotic mechanisms (such as mathematical symbols, diagrams, gesture) provide the means for ideas to be talked through and communicated between individuals on the social plane. Following the process of internalisation and personal reconstruction by the individual, language and other semiotic modes provide the tools for individual thinking. In this way talk and thought are seen as being intimately related.

Drawing upon Bakhtin's ideas (Holquist 1981), we might say that learning science involves learning the *social language* of science. This social language is the product of the scientific community, a distinctive way of talking and thinking about the natural world, which must be consistent with the phenomena of that world. Learning science therefore involves being introduced to the language of the scientific community and this can be achieved only through the agency of a teacher or some other knowledgeable figure. Science is not there to be discovered through close scrutiny of the natural world. Furthermore, the scientific perspective is not necessarily the same as *everyday ways* of talking and thinking about natural phenomena. For example, the notion that 'plants get food from the soil' (common in everyday social language) differs from the scientific point of view (where plants synthesise carbohydrates from water and atmospheric carbon dioxide). The informal or spontaneous concepts (Vygotsky 1934) that constitute an everyday social language include many of those ideas that are referred to as alternative conceptions or misconceptions in the science education literature (Leach and Scott 2002).

We see teaching and learning science as involving an introduction to the social language of school science against a 'backdrop' of everyday reasoning. This theoretical perspective frames our approach to planning and implementing science teaching. Although the perspective is based upon scholarship, and has been subjected to scrutiny from other researchers, it can not really be viewed as *evidence*. Indeed, although there are studies in the literature which present evidence that is most plausibly explained by a social constructivist perspective on learning, we find it hard to imagine how this (or any) perspective on learning might be 'proved' through empirical evaluation. Rather, the perspective provides a lens though which research evidence can be interpreted and drawn upon in the design and evaluation of science teaching.

An approach to planning teaching interventions

In the following sections, we show how we used the social constructivist perspective on learning to interpret research evidence, in designing the three teaching interventions.

Students' 'everyday' reasoning about natural phenomena

The pioneering work of Jean Piaget, in the early part of the twentieth century, established that there are commonalities in children's everyday accounts of the natural world. For most school science topic areas, the research literature on teaching and learning science now contains several studies (and some review articles) on learners' likely reasoning about the topic prior to teaching – and on how that reasoning changes as a result of teaching. We shall refer to this as the learners' *everyday reasoning*. The literature may also highlight common difficulties and misunderstandings that learners develop *during* teaching within the topic domain.

In relation to the three topic areas focused on in this study, the following examples illustrate the kind of evidence about students' everyday reasoning that was found in the research literature:

- *Simple electric circuits*: 'Electricity' (which is not differentiated into clear and distinct ideas of charge, current, energy) is thought to leave a battery (the source) and move around the circuit in a temporal sequence, with the result that there is a pause between connecting a circuit and observing behaviour such as a bulb lighting, and that its effect is 'used up' by each component in turn as it passes through (for example, Shipstone 1988).
- *Plant nutrition*: Plants are thought to ingest their food 'ready-made' in a similar way to animals. When students encounter teaching about photosynthesis, they often retain a model of food as ingested

through the roots, and find it implausible that biomass in plants is synthesised mainly from water and carbon dioxide (for example, Bell 1984).

- *Particles and change*: Matter is thought of as being continuous rather than particulate. When students encounter simple particulate models of matter through teaching, they often assume that particles are tiny bits of the substance itself, with the same properties (such as melting or expanding) (for example, Driver *et al.* 1994).

Learning demand

Such insights into learners' everyday reasoning provide a starting point for thinking about the design of teaching interventions. Building on this starting point, we have developed the notion of *learning demand* (Leach and Scott 1995, 2002) to characterise more precisely the intellectual task faced by learners in coming to understand the scientific account of a given topic. The learning demand characterises the ways in which the scientific account (or more specifically the 'school science' view) of a particular natural phenomenon, differs from everyday views of that phenomenon. For example, in the context of teaching and learning about air pressure, students typically draw upon the everyday concept of suction in explaining phenomena, whilst the scientific point of view is based upon differences in air pressure, with the high pressure region (often the atmosphere) being the agent of change. There is an obvious difference here in the *conceptual tools* used to develop explanations.

Learning demands can also arise from differences in the *epistemological* framing of explanations. Thus, the ways of generating explanations using scientific models and theories that are taken for granted in school science are not part of the everyday ways of talking and thinking of most learners (Vosniadou 1994; Driver *et al.* 1996). Whilst in science, great importance is attached to developing a small number of models and theories, which can be applied generally to as broad a range of phenomena as possible, the same is not true for everyday explanations. Thus, in science, energy is an absolutely central concept, simply because it offers a generalisable way of thinking about virtually any phenomenon. In everyday contexts, there is not the same attention to generalisability, and the term 'energy' might be used with different meanings in different contexts.

Finally, learning demands may result from differences in the *ontology* of the conceptual tools used (Chi 1992; Vosniadou 1994). Thus, entities that are taken for granted as having a real existence in the realm of school science may not be similarly referred to in the everyday language of students. For example, there is evidence that when many lower secondary school students are introduced to the concept of matter cycling in ecosystems, they do not think about atmospheric gases as a potential source of matter for the chemical processes of ecological systems (Leach *et al.* 1996). There is a learning issue here, which relates to the students' basic commitments about the nature of matter – initially they do not consider gases to be substantive. Similarly, 'energy' in science is regarded as an abstract mathematical device, whilst in everyday contexts it is often referred to as being substantial in nature: 'coal contains energy'; 'I've run out of energy'. In coming to understand the scientific concept of energy, students must therefore come to appreciate that energy is not *material*: rather, it is an abstract concept. It belongs to a different ontological category.

From this point of view, learning science involves coming to terms with the conceptual tools, and associated epistemology and ontology, of school science. If the differences between school science and everyday ways of reasoning are great, because there is little overlap between the concepts and associated epistemology and ontology of school science and everyday views, then the topic in question appears difficult to learn and to teach. Conversely, if there is considerable overlap between school science and everyday views, the learning demand is small and students may think that the school science account is 'easy' or 'obvious'.

At this point it is worth reflecting for a moment on the nature of the evidence which we are using in this part of the planning of the teaching intervention. The concept of learning demand itself follows from the social constructivist perspective on learning in setting up the comparison between everyday and school science views. Actually identifying learning demands involves drawing on research evidence about students' domain-specific reasoning about natural phenomena. This evidence is empirical, based on students' written or oral responses to research questions, and much of it has been replicated through multiple studies around the world. The concept of learning demand therefore provides a bridge between findings of empirical research on students' reasoning, and the design of teaching interventions.

Identification of teaching goals

Having identified the learning demands for each of the three teaching interventions, we then considered how these demands might be addressed through teaching. We started by identifying a set of *teaching goals* for each intervention. The teaching goals make explicit the ways in which the students' ideas and understandings are to be worked on through the intervention and guidance of the teacher. Once the teaching goals have been clarified, attention can be given to considering what teaching activities might be used to address these goals. The overall approach to planning is therefore based on the following overall scheme:

1.   Identify the *school science* knowledge to be taught.
2.   Consider how this area of science is conceptualised in the *everyday* reasoning of students.
3.   Identify the *learning demand* by appraising the nature of any differences (conceptual, epistemological, ontological) between 1 and 2.
4.   Design a *teaching intervention* to address each aspect of this learning demand:
     a)   identifying the *teaching goals* for each phase of the intervention
     b)   planning a sequence of *activities* to address the specific teaching goals
     c)   specifying how these teaching activities might be linked to appropriate *forms of classroom communication*.

We shall say more about the last point, relating to forms of classroom communication, shortly. First, however, we turn to illustrating this approach to planning for the treatment of content in teaching interventions by focusing on the example of simple electric circuits.

Planning a teaching intervention: Simple electric circuits

Step 1: School science knowledge to be taught

In the context of the national curriculum for science in England (DfEE/QCA 1999), the school science knowledge to be taught involves developing a model of energy transfer via an electric current where:

*   the current in a series circuit depends on the number of cells and the number and nature of other components.
*   current is not 'used up' by components.
*   energy is transferred from batteries and other sources to other components in electrical circuits.

This model is developed in subsequent phases of the national curriculum by introducing the concept of voltage.

Step 2: Students' everyday views about electric circuits

A review of the literature on teaching and learning about simple electric circuits was conducted and the following characteristic patterns in students' reasoning were identified (see, for example, Psillos 1998, Shipstone 1988):

- The circuit is not viewed as a *whole system*, with changes occurring virtually simultaneously in all parts (for example, when a switch is closed, charges are set into motion in all parts of the circuit together). Instead, students often explain effects in terms of *sequential* models, where any disturbance travels in one direction, affecting circuit components in succession. Thus, when an extra resistive component (such as a bulb) is added in series to a circuit, students often predict that the 'first component' after the battery gets most, or all, of the energy.
- Students often think about electric circuits in terms of a *source* (the battery) and a *consumer* (for example, a bulb). This can lead to problems:
  - the charge which constitutes an electric current is considered to originate in the battery (the *source*)
  - the battery is considered to provide a fixed electric current
  - when an extra battery is added to a circuit the extra current is thought to come from the additional battery (the *source*)
  - electric current and energy are not differentiated, with students suggesting that the current is used up in a bulb (the *consumer*).
- The size of the electric current is estimated to be less in high resistance parts of a circuit (such as a bulb filament) than in other parts (such as the connecting leads).

In relation to broader epistemological issues, it is likely that the students will have little experience of using a scientific model which involves moving between the 'theoretical world' of the model (based on the abstract concepts of charge, current and energy) and the 'real world' of observations and measurements (Tiberghien 1996). They are also likely to have little appreciation of the fact that scientific models are intended to be applied generally to a wide range of contexts (Driver *et al.* 1996).

Step 3: Identification of learning demands

By comparing the school science and everyday views identified above, the following learning demands were developed. Learning in this area involves the students in coming to:

*   develop abstract scientific concepts of charge, current, resistance and energy in the context of explaining the behaviour of simple electric circuits
*   understand that the battery is the source of energy for the circuit
*   understand that energy is transferred in the circuit and not the current
*   understand that the charges originate in the circuit and not in the battery
*   understand that an electric circuit behaves as a whole system, such that a change in one part of the circuit affects all other parts of the circuit simultaneously
*   understand that the electric circuit model based on concepts of charge, current, resistance and energy can be used to predict and explain the behaviour of a wide range of simple circuits.

The first five elements of the learning demand involve conceptual issues whilst the final element relates to more general epistemological matters.

Step 4: Designing the teaching intervention

Teaching goals

The first step in designing the teaching intervention involved formulating a set of teaching goals, which were based on the learning demands and specified more directly the nature of the pedagogical interventions to be taken by the teacher. The first set of teaching goals is conceptual:
    To *build on* the ideas that:

*   batteries make things work
*   electricity/current flows.

To *introduce, and support the development of*, the ideas that:

*   an electric current consists of a flow of charge
*   the electric current provides the means for transferring energy

- components such as bulbs introduce resistance to the circuit. The resistance restricts the flow of charge, reducing the current flowing around the whole circuit and causing energy transfer as the charge passes through the resistance.

To *draw attention to, and to emphasise,* the idea that:

- the battery is the energy source for the circuit
- the charges originate in the circuit and not solely in the battery
- the electric current does not get used up
- it is energy which is transferred in resistances.

To *emphasise throughout* that:

- electric circuits behave as whole systems, such that a change in one part of the circuit affects all other parts of the circuit simultaneously.

Progressively to *differentiate between*:

- the theoretical concepts of charge, current, energy: emphasising that the electric current does not get used up, rather it is energy which is transferred in resistances to the surroundings.

The second set of teaching goals is epistemological:
  To *introduce, and support the development of,* the idea that:

- the electric circuit model based on concepts of charge, current, resistance and energy can be used to predict and explain the behaviour of a wide range of simple circuits.

It is instructive to compare this list of detailed teaching goals with what is typically presented to teachers in curriculum specifications (see Step 1). Curriculum specifications typically provide information about 'what is to be taught' at a macro level. In contrast, the teaching goals derived from research evidence (through the learning demand analysis) provide a much more fine-grained analysis of the learning points which need to be addressed by the teacher.

Planning a sequence of activities

The teaching intervention was designed to address the teaching goals listed above and consists of four lessons. In Lesson 1, two diagnostic questions (from the banks developed in the work discussed in Chapters 3 and 6) were set for the students to work through individually, with a view to the teacher being able to probe their initial understandings of a simple electric circuit. The teacher then introduces a starter activity involving a 'Big Circuit'. This is a simple circuit including a battery and bulb, which stretches all of the way around the laboratory. The students are asked to predict what will happen when the Big Circuit is completed. This activity was designed to challenge student thinking about the 'battery as source' (as identified through the learning demand analysis) and debates typically ensue in class on whether the bulb will light 'straightaway' or 'after a short time'. Completing the circuit shows that the bulb lights 'immediately' and attention is then turned to developing a model to account for this finding: 'What is going on inside the circuit to allow this to happen?'

The basic elements of the electric circuit model are introduced via a teaching analogy. The approach taken in the teaching intervention emphasises the importance of introducing the teaching analogy *systematically*, making explicit links between the home and target domains (Glynn *et al.* 1995). Given the importance of making clear links to the analogy, it was decided that rather than include a number of different teaching analogies in the intervention (each of which would demand careful introduction and development), the focus would be on just one.

The particular teaching analogy selected addresses the key teaching goal of differentiating between charge and energy. In the analogy the electric circuit is represented by a continuous line of vans (charges), collecting loaves of bread (energy) at a bakery, and carrying them round to a supermarket (bulb) where they are delivered and dissipated. There has been considerable debate in the literature about the advantages and disadvantages of specific teaching analogies, in the context of electric circuits (see, for example, Schwedes and Dudeck 1996). We recognise that charges-carrying-energy analogies have their drawbacks, relating in particular to the detail of what happens during the transient phases after a circuit is completed or broken, to how well they can account for the behaviour of circuits with several loads, and whether they introduce distracting ideas about variations in the speed of the carriers. We came to the conclusion, however, that such weaknesses are unlikely to be detrimental to student progress during the first steps of developing an electric circuit model.

Although many of the activities used in the teaching intervention look similar to activities used in many science classrooms, it is worth underlining how the teaching intervention differed from the approaches typically used in British classrooms. Perhaps the most significant difference is the proportion of time devoted to important issues in students' learning through activities such as the 'Big Circuit', in comparison to typical teaching approaches. Furthermore, the overall intervention was designed so that the same teaching analogy was used throughout the four lessons, as the teacher supported the students in coming to understand the effects of changing the numbers of cells and bulbs on the electric current and energy transfer. Time was spent systematically developing the analogy and showing how it relates to actual circuits and to a scientific model of the behaviour of circuits, and students were provided with the opportunity to use the scientific model and analogy to generate explanations. Although analogies are often used by British science teachers when introducing simple explanations of electric circuits, they are rarely built up and used systematically to bridge between a scientific model and real circuits. The teaching activities also address the epistemological teaching goal of coming to appreciate the generalisability of scientific models by demonstrating the consistent application of one model to a range of contexts. It is not typical for British science teachers to address the way in which models are used to generate explanations of electric circuits.

Planning the sequence of activities involved using a number of different sources of research evidence. Some of this evidence relates to general pedagogical perspectives, such as the use of analogies and formative assessment (Black and Wiliam 1998a, 1998b) whilst other evidence is taken from studies which focus directly on teaching and learning about electric circuits. What precisely do these sources of evidence tell us? In relation to use of analogies, the general perspectives provide helpful advice about issues that need to be addressed whatever the context (such as the systematic introduction of the analogy and careful linkage to the target case). The studies relating specifically to electric circuits offer discussions of the pros and cons of particular analogies (in relation to the physics subject matter), details about the use of particular analogies in classroom settings and, in some cases, sets of data relating to student learning. What these teaching studies do *not* provide is any kind of appraisal of the *relative* effectiveness of different analogies in supporting student learning.

Thinking about classroom communication

In the preceding sections we have set out a general approach to designing teaching interventions and have illustrated this approach in relation to the intervention on electric circuits. A further aspect of the design relates to different modes of *classroom communication*.

As outlined earlier, from a social constructivist perspective on teaching and learning the teacher has a central role to play in introducing the scientific perspective and providing opportunities for students to begin to 'talk and think' the science for themselves. It is with these views in mind that the decision was taken to plan teaching activities not only in terms of what the teacher and students would be *doing*, but also in relation to the kind of *talking* involved. Thus at some times the teacher might be making a demonstration where the teaching goal is to introduce new ideas. At other times the class might be engaged in a brainstorming activity where the teaching goal is to bring student ideas out into the open. The nature of the talk involved in each of these scenarios is quite different and we wanted to specify, as far as is possible, what was intended for each activity. In this way, attending to the nature of the classroom talk was integrated into the teaching design process.

Communicative approach

In order to specify the different kinds of talk to be developed with different teaching activities, we drew upon a framework based on the concept of *communicative approach*, developed from sociocultural theory to interpret transcripts of classroom talk (Mortimer and Scott 2003). Mortimer and Scott identify four classes of communicative approach, by characterising the talk between teacher and students along each of two dimensions: *interactive/non-interactive* and *dialogic/authoritative*.

The teacher–student talk can be *interactive* in the sense of allowing for the participation of more than one person (teacher interacting with students), or *non-interactive* in the sense of excluding the participation of other people (teacher making presentation to students). The teacher–student talk can be *dialogic* in the sense that the teacher attends to the students' points of view as well as to the school science view. Alternatively, the teacher might focus on just one point of view with an *authoritative* approach and here there is no exploration of different ideas.

Combining the two dimensions, any sequence of classroom talk can be identified as being either *interactive* or *non-interactive* on the one hand, and *dialogic* or *authoritative* on the other (although, in practice, some classroom sequences entail aspects of both dialogic and authoritative talk). This gives rise to four classes of communicative approach (Figure 4.1). In planning each teaching activity to address a specific teaching goal, the nature of the intended 'talk around the activity' was framed in terms of these four classes of communicative approach. In preparing the teaching schemes, the intended type of talk was indicated using of a system of icons, as shown in Figure 4.2.

'Presenting' involves either lecturing (*non-interactive/authoritative*) or a series of teacher-led questions and answers (*interactive/authoritative*). 'Discussing/probing' involves *interactive/dialogic*

	INTERACTIVE	NON-INTERACTIVE
DIALOGIC	**A: Interactive/ Dialogic**: the teacher seeks to elicit and explore students' ideas about a particular issue with a series of 'genuine' questions.	**B: Non-interactive/ Dialogic**: the teacher is in presentational mode (*non-interactive*), but explicitly considers and draws attention to different points of view (*dialogic*), possibly in providing a summary of an earlier discussion.
AUTHORITATIVE	**C: Interactive/ Authoritative**: the teacher typically leads students through a sequence of instructional questions and answers with the aim of reaching one specific point of view.	**D: Non-interactive/ Authoritative**: the teacher presents a specific point of view.

Figure 4.1 Four classes of communicative approach

		The purpose of the talk	How and when it happens
Presenting		You are introducing or reviewing **new ideas.**	This may be through a presentation by you or by whole-class discussion led by you.
Discussing/probing		You are finding out about the students' ideas and understandings.	this may be through asking open questions, 'what do you think?' in whole-class or small group situations.
Supporting		You are supporting the students as they talk about their developing ideas, using key questions and offering appropriate responses to their questions	This is likely to be achieved as the students are working on paired or small group activities.

Figure 4.2 Icons to indicate the intended type of talk

discourse. 'Supporting' involves the teacher working with small groups of students and using both *interactive/dialogic* and *interactive/ authoritative* discourse.

What can we say about the origins and nature of these ideas relating to classroom communication? The concept of communicative approach (Mortimer and Scott 2003) is based on the theoretical distinction made by Bakhtin (1934) between authoritative and internally persuasive discourse (Wertsch 1991). In this respect, communicative approach is a form of theory-based planning tool. However, the distinction between authoritative and dialogic discourse has been used, in a number of studies, as a basis for classifying classroom interactions (see, for example, Alexander 2004, Mortimer 1998) and to this extent there is some empirical evidence for the validity of using these ideas to characterise interactions in science classrooms. What is not currently available, however, is much evidence about the impact of utilising different kinds of talk on student learning. Some studies have been carried out in this area (see, for example, Rojas-Drummond and Mercer 2004), but the evidence is very limited.

From research evidence-informed design to classroom action

In the previous sections we have set out a research evidence-informed approach to designing teaching interventions which moves from an analysis of content to the development of teaching activities and the nature of the talk around those activities.

This approach to identifying teaching goals is strongly informed by research evidence. However, it is important to recognise that the process of developing teaching activities inevitably involves judgements about selecting one activity rather than another, and that this step is less well informed by research evidence to evaluate different approaches (Figure 4.3). In developing teaching activities, it is also clear that effective lessons must motivate both students and teachers and conform to their expectations of what 'good' science lessons look like. No matter how 'research evidence-informed' a teaching activity is, if it is perceived as being dull, it is unlikely to prompt engagement of students and meaningful learning.

In order to move from research evidence-informed teaching goals to sequences of lessons ready for the classroom, we therefore worked with a group of nine teachers (who constituted the Development Phase group, see Appendix), three from each main science discipline. These Development Phase teachers attended planning meetings at the

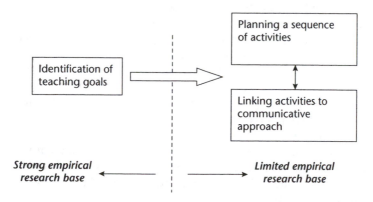

Figure 4.3 Using research evidence to inform the design of teaching

university where they contributed their professional knowledge (see Chapter 1) to discussions about teaching activities to address specific teaching goals. In some cases the teachers suggested possible activities and at other times offered feedback on ideas proposed by the research team. The contribution of the teachers involved creative insight and professional knowledge about 'what would work', rather than knowledge of research and scholarship on teaching and learning science, which came chiefly from the researchers. The researchers involved had all also had extensive experience in the past as classroom teachers, which they also brought to bear on the design.

What kinds of insights were used?

Looking back over this account, it is instructive to return to the question of what different insights, including research evidence, were employed in designing the teaching interventions, and what was the source of each kind of insight. The range of insights used is summarised in Figure 4.4.

The three teaching interventions as 'worked examples'

The point has already been made that the use of research evidence cannot lead to unique teaching solutions. There will always be more than one way of addressing a particular teaching goal and the approach taken is likely to vary with the nature and history of specific teachers working with particular classes. It is quite common (and often entirely legitimate) for individual teachers to say, 'I could never do that with my class'. We therefore view our teaching schemes as 'worked examples' which demonstrate *one* approach to addressing research evidence-informed teaching goals, through teaching interventions which are themselves research evidence-informed.

A final point that we would wish to emphasise is the *fundamental* importance of being clear about teaching goals, as already discussed in Chapter 3. It seems to us that one of the clear strengths of the research evidence-informed approach to planning outlined here is the detailed analysis leading to the identification of teaching goals. Through this kind of analysis the 'conceptual terrain' of the teaching and learning domain is laid out and the teacher becomes more aware of what is involved for the students in learning in this area and what the teacher might do to support that learning.

Insight	Source of insight
1. Theoretical framing perspective	
A social constructivist perspective on teaching and learning science	Scholarly writing in the academic literature on teaching and learning
2. Planning tools	
Learning demand	Developed from a social constructivist perspective on learning and teaching, and knowledge of the existence of research evidence about students' reasoning
Communicative approach	Scholarly writing in the academic literature
	Empirically validated as an *analytical* tool (but not as a *planning* tool leading to enhanced learning)
3. Students' reasoning	Multiple (and frequently replicated) empirical studies
4. Design of teaching interventions	
General pedagogical perspectives	Reflective articles, position papers, analytical accounts in science education and psychological research
Teaching and learning specific topics	Classroom-based empirical studies, but with limited comparative evaluation of learning data
Teachers' professional knowledge	See Chapter 1, Figure 1.1

Figure 4.4 Insights informing the design of the teaching interventions

Summary

In this chapter, we have shown in some detail how research evidence and scholarly perspectives on learning were used to inform the design of three teaching interventions, as well as identifying other necessary influences upon the design. We have argued that, rather than being unique solutions to the problems of teaching effectively the ideas which each is addressing, these teaching interventions are 'worked examples' of research evidence-informed design principles. The interventions demonstrate the interplay between general design principles or criteria, and issues and choices that are specific to the subject content with which the intervention is concerned.

Chapter 5

Implementing and evaluating teaching interventions
Towards research evidence-based practice?

In Chapter 4, we described how we designed three short teaching interventions, drawing explicitly on insights from research on science learning in specific conceptual domains, and theoretical perspectives on teaching and learning science. A group of teachers worked with the research team, bringing their professional expertise to the development process. We argued in Chapter 4 that the teaching emerging from the use of these short interventions was an example of research evidence-informed practice. In this chapter we turn our attention to the implementation and evaluation of these teaching interventions, to see if they achieve the intended learning outcomes better than other ways of teaching the same ideas. If the results suggest this to be the case, we then want to ask if it can reasonably be claimed that future implementations of the teaching interventions are examples of research evidence-based practice.

Introduction

The three teaching interventions described in Chapter 4 were designed to address two overarching aims. The first of these was to develop students' conceptual understanding in specific topic areas so that the learning outcomes were measurably better than those achieved by students following their school's usual scheme of work. The second aim was for the teaching interventions to be usable by teachers not involved in their development, leading to similar enhanced learning gains (with minimal training). This second aim, it seems to us, is central to any

Authored by John Leach, Phil Scott, Jaume Ametller, Andy Hind and Jenny Lewis

argument that a teaching approach should be more generally adopted: there has to be some evidence that the positive effects of the teaching approach can be *transferred* from the site of development. Our evaluation of the teaching interventions therefore addressed the following questions:

- Did students who were taught using the designed teaching interventions develop conceptual understanding that was consistent with the aims of the teaching? Did students achieve measurably better conceptual understanding than comparable students following their school's usual scheme of work? Were there any differences in learning outcomes for students taught by teachers who had been involved in the design of the teaching (the Development Phase teachers) and those who had not (the Transfer Phase teachers)?
- To what extent was the teaching as implemented consistent with the design principles of the teaching interventions as described in Chapter 4?

Our evaluation of the teaching interventions was not designed to investigate causal mechanisms for any improvements in students' attainment that were noted. Nonetheless, we wanted to have evidence of how the teaching was implemented in order to evaluate the plausibility of different possible explanations of any improvements. We also draw upon evidence from the evaluation in considering whether future implementations of the teaching interventions might be judged to be research evidence-based practice.

Evaluating the teaching interventions in terms of students' conceptual understanding

To address the first set of evaluation questions (which ask whether students attained conceptual understanding consistent with the aims of the teaching), we used a number of short diagnostic questions focusing upon key conceptual content. The majority of these questions were administered both before and after teaching, although in some cases we did not judge it appropriate to ask students certain questions prior to teaching. For example, it did not seem sensible to ask questions about the readings on ammeters prior to teaching students what an ammeter is. Some of the questions were set in contexts that were covered in the teaching interventions, whilst others were designed to test students' ability in applying concepts in novel situations. In addition to responding to the questions directly after teaching, the students also completed the same questions around three months later, in order to give an indication of the extent to which conceptual understanding had been retained over time.

In this way, the diagnostic questions were used to make an *internal* evaluation of the teaching, establishing the extent to which students' learning was consistent with the aims of the teaching. However, evidence from an internal evaluation cannot be used to compare and evaluate different teaching practices. Therefore, an *external* evaluation of the teaching was also carried out to ascertain whether the students' learning was any better than that achieved through the usual teaching approaches. This involved comparing the conceptual understanding of the students who followed the designed interventions (as measured with the diagnostic questions) with the performance of other students *in the same school* who had followed the school's usual teaching programme. Evidence from the external evaluation was used to inform a judgement about the effectiveness of the designed teaching intervention in promoting students' understanding, compared with the teaching approaches normally used in their schools.

Methodologically, such external comparisons are extremely difficult to make. For example, imagine that two groups of students follow different teaching interventions about plant nutrition and that, after teaching, group A achieves significantly better diagnostic test results than group B. One possible explanation for this is that the teaching followed by group A was better in some respect than that followed by group B. Alternatively, students in group A might have been more able than those in B, or they may have started the teaching with much better understanding than those in group B. To minimise these possibilities, we asked schools to match the classes following the designed teaching intervention (the Experimental classes) to classes of similar ability, who had followed a similar curriculum in the past, and who were now following the school's usual teaching scheme (the Baseline classes). Baseline classes completed the same test items as the Experimental classes and data were included in comparisons between Experimental and Baseline classes only if there was no significant difference in students' scores on the pre-test.

In comparing the performances of the Experimental and Baseline classes, it was also recognised that the diagnostic questions used to assess the students' learning might have been biased towards the content or style of the teaching followed by the Experimental classes. In our study, we tried to minimise this possibility by asking the Development Phase teachers to confirm that the content of the designed interventions matched closely with what is normally taught in schools, and with the national curriculum for England. In some cases, on reviewing test data and conducting post-teaching interviews with teachers, it was clear that the content addressed in Baseline classes was significantly different from that in the designed interventions. Such data were eliminated from comparisons, because of an obvious testing bias.

Another possible source of bias in reviewing differences between students' attainment in the Experimental and Baseline classes relates to the teachers themselves. The Development Phase teachers had been identified as skilled and motivated classroom practitioners, and each of them had invested significant time and thought in the design of the teaching interventions. By contrast, the teachers who taught the Baseline classes were a convenience sample, selected on the basis that they taught classes of similar ability to those following the designed interventions. Intuitively, one would *expect* better results from students in classes taught by skilled teachers who are enthusiastic stakeholders in a new teaching intervention which is being tested for the first time. In order to investigate the extent to which any gains in attainment, achieved by Experimental classes over Baseline classes, could be reproduced by teachers not involved in the design of the teaching, we recruited a further sample of teachers to implement the designed interventions. These Transfer Phase teachers had no connection with the project at all. They were recommended to us by local science advisory teachers and in most cases were not known by members of the research team. We collected test data from students in these Transfer classes before and after teaching with the designed interventions, using the same diagnostic questions, and from students in similar classes in the same schools following the schools' usual programmes of study.

The ideal research design to investigate our questions would involve the random allocation of students to 'intervention' and 'control' groups, and the random allocation of 'intervention' and 'control' groups across schools. This was not feasible, however, given that schools are not in a position to manage or support such major changes in their ways of operating.

The chemistry teaching intervention was significantly different in structure from the two other interventions. It aimed to revise and extend students' understanding of the use of a simple particulate model of matter to account for physical and chemical change processes, rather than introduce ideas about physical and chemical change for the first time. It was not possible, however, to identify Baseline classes covering similar content to the designed teaching intervention, and we have not therefore drawn upon data relating to the chemistry teaching intervention in this chapter.

Findings from the diagnostic questions

In addition to the nine Development Phase teachers (three biology, three chemistry, three physics), nine teachers (four biology, five physics) were involved in teaching the designed interventions in the Transfer Phase. The Transfer Phase teachers taught in schools of similar profile to those of the Development Phase teachers (ranging from affluent outer suburban areas to the inner city). Information about the full sample of teachers and classes for both Phases is presented in Table 5.1.

Table 5.1   Sample information

		Reference	Number of students	
			Experimental class[1]	Baseline class
Development Phase	Biology	BDV	27	27
		BDC	28	30
		BDS	29	See note 2
	Physics	PDA	20	20
		PDD1	29	22
		PDD2	28	22
		PDS	23	26
Transfer Phase	Biology	BTC	26	21
		BTF	26	28
		BTP	29	28
		BTT	22	29
	Physics	PTM	24	29
		PTL	26	23
		PTR	25	23
		PTT	21	23
		PTK	26	23

Notes
1   n refers to the number of students responding to the diagnostic questions after the implementation (post-test).
2   No valid Baseline data were available; BDS has therefore been omitted from the sample.

The diagnostic questions used to evaluate students' conceptual understanding are mostly in two parts. The first part involves making a prediction of some kind (such as the brightness of bulbs in a simple circuit), and this is followed by an opportunity for students to explain their prediction. Two examples of questions of this type are shown in Chapter 3, Figures 3.1 and 3.2. Students' responses were coded according to whether they made a correct prediction or not, and the extent to which their explanation drew upon the target conceptual knowledge of the teaching intervention. Here, we present findings from the pre- and post-tests completed by students in both Experimental and Baseline groups, from both the Development and Transfer Phases. We have not included data from the delayed post-tests. This is because, in a significant number of cases, it was apparent that students in either Baseline or Experimental groups had undertaken further related study in their science courses between the end of teaching and the implementation of the delayed post-tests.

The biology teaching intervention

Three questions were used to evaluate students' conceptual under-standing of plant nutrition. Table 5.2 shows data for these questions which relate to the predictions made by students and to the ways in which they used the model introduced in the teaching to frame explanations. After coding whether students' predictions were correct or not, their explanations were categorised into three groups:

- Responses broadly consistent with the scientific model introduced in the teaching ('Consistent')
- Responses that are consistent with the taught model but incomplete in some respect ('Incomplete')
- Other responses ('Other').

These coded responses were averaged across the three questions. For example, in case study BDV, the post-test figure of 8.3 students with 'consistent use of the model' indicates that, out of a group of 27 students answering three questions, the mean number using a complete model consistent with that taught was 8.3. This in turn represents 30.6 per cent of the total number of students.

In each of the pairs of Experimental and associated Baseline groups in Table 5.2, analysis of pre-test results using a standard statistical test (χ^2) suggests that there is no significant difference in levels of

Table 5.2 Number of students (and percentage of class in italics) giving responses of different types following implementation of the biology teaching intervention

Phase	Case study	Pre-test				Post-test (prediction)				Post-test (use of the model)			
		n	Consistent	Incomplete	Other	n	Consistent	Incomplete	Other	n	Consistent	Incomplete	Other
Development Phase	BDV	27	6.3	5.0	15.7	27	21.0	2.0	4.0	27	8.3	8.3	10.5
			23.5	*18.5*	*58.0*		*77.8*	*7.4*	*14.8*		*30.6*	*30.6*	*38.9*
	Base	27	7.7	6.7	12.7	23	14.0	3.0	6.0	23	1.8	6.0	15.3
			28.4	*24.7*	*46.9*		*60.9*	*13.0*	*26.1*		*7.6*	*26.1*	*66.3*
	BDC	28	10.3	7.7	10.0	28	24.0	2.0	2.0	28	18.0	6.8	3.3
			36.9	*27.4*	*35.7*		*85.7*	*7.1*	*7.1*		*64.3*	*24.1*	*11.6*
	Base	30	8.0	14.0	8.0	29	26.0	2.0	1.0	29	7.5	11.3	10.3
			26.7	*46.7*	*26.7*		*89.7*	*6.9*	*3.4*		*25.9*	*38.8*	*35.3*
Transfer Phase	BTC	18	7.3	1.7	9.0	26	21.0	0.0	5.0	26	4.0	9.0	13.1
			40.7	*9.3*	*50.0*		*80.8*	*0.0*	*19.2*		*15.4*	*34.6*	*50.0*
	Base	30	11.3	4.0	14.6	21	16.0	0.0	5.0	21	1.3	4.0	15.8
			37.8	*13.3*	*48.8*		*76.2*	*0.0*	*23.8*		*6.0*	*19.0*	*75.0*
	BTF	23	8.0	2.3	12.7	26	21.0	4.0	1.0	26	5.3	7.3	13.5
			34.8	*10.1*	*55.0*		*80.8*	*15.4*	*3.8*		*20.2*	*27.9*	*51.9*
	Base	21	6.0	1.3	13.7	28	24.0	2.0	2.0	28	2.3	4.3	21.6
			28.6	*6.3*	*65.1*		*85.7*	*7.1*	*7.1*		*8.0*	*15.2*	*76.8*
	BTP	29	8.7	4.3	16.0	29	22.0	4.0	3.0	29	6.5	6.3	16.3
			29.9	*14.9*	*55.1*		*75.9*	*13.8*	*10.3*		*22.4*	*21.6*	*56.0*
	Base	30	13.0	4.7	12.3	28	25.0	0.0	3.0	28	15.0	5.3	7.8
			43.3	*15.6*	*41.1*		*89.3*	*0.0*	*10.7*		*53.6*	*18.8*	*27.7*
	BTT	26	5.0	5.3	15.7	22	14.0	0.0	8.0	22	3.3	5.0	13.8
			19.2	*20.5*	*60.2*		*63.6*	*0.0*	*36.3*		*14.8*	*22.7*	*62.5*
	Base	28	3.7	3.7	20.6	29	25.0	0.0	4.0	29	0.5	3.3	25.3
			13.1	*13.1*	*73.8*		*86.2*	*0.0*	*13.7*		*1.7*	*11.2*	*87.1*

students' attainment on diagnostic questions about plant nutrition prior to teaching. We have therefore assumed that it is legitimate to use these pairs of case studies in making comparisons. First, we compared the performance of students in Experimental and Baseline groups on making predictions requiring knowledge of photosynthesis. A standard statistical test for data of this sort (χ^2) indicates that the differences observed, between the Experimental and Baseline groups, are not large enough to suggest that the effect is due to factors other than chance and random variation. We cannot therefore conclude that students who followed the intervention were better than other students at making predictions. However, results from a comparison of the performance of students in using the model of plant nutrition taught in the teaching scheme to frame explanations tell a different story. In all cases except one (BTP), more students in Experimental groups than in Baseline groups used the taught model of plant nutrition in answering questions, to an extent that is very unlikely simply to reflect random variation. (A possible explanation for the exception is that the teaching of the Baseline class in BTP addressed many of the learning demands identified for the designed teaching intervention, and incorporated a very high level of interactive talk, even though the teacher had not seen the designed teaching intervention.)

There is considerable variability in the extent to which students in Experimental and Baseline groups used the model of photosynthesis after teaching. However, it is possible to get some sense of differences between the Development and Transfer Phases. We added together the numbers of students whose use of the model of plant nutrition was coded as either consistent or incomplete, and then compared the difference in the mean number in the Experimental and Baseline groups in the Development and Transfer Phases. Using this approach, responses from students in the Experimental groups in the Development Phase were coded consistent or incomplete 25.6 per cent more often than responses from students in Baseline groups. In the Transfer Phase, the comparable figure is 11.6 per cent if class BTP is included, and 24.5 per cent if BTP is omitted. Once BTP is omitted, there is no significant difference between students' results in the Development and Transfer Phases. This leads us to conclude that teachers not involved in developing the teaching interventions can nonetheless use them, with the result that students' understanding is significantly better than would be expected if the students had followed the school's usual teaching approach.

The physics teaching intervention

We now turn our attention to the physics teaching intervention. Table 5.3 shows students' results for the pre- and post-tests. Students' responses to the two pre-test questions and six post-test questions were coded and conflated in a similar way to the biology questions. The number and percentage of students making correct and incorrect predictions are presented, along with numbers and percentages of those using an explanatory model consistent with the scientific view, those using an incomplete explanation and other responses. Classes PDD1 and PDD2 were from the same school and are compared to the same Baseline data. The same applies to classes PTL, PTR, PTT and PTK, which were all taken from another single school.

We have included all pairs of Experimental and Baseline groups listed in Table 5.3 in comparisons, as there is no statistically significant difference in the groups' performances in the pre-test on explanations (based upon the use of similar statistical tests to those used for the biology case studies). However, Experimental groups PDD1 and PDD2 were significantly better at predicting the behaviour of electric circuits than the Baseline group. Nevertheless, we decided to keep Experimental groups PDD1 and PDD2 in the sample because teachers in the school did not consider that these classes were more able than the Baseline group. In any case, making predictions about the behaviour of electric circuits in the absence of explanations did not feature in the aims of the designed teaching intervention (or in the English national curriculum for science, though questions requiring such predictions are used in national tests). There were no significant differences between the predictions about the behaviour of electric circuits made by other Experimental and Baseline groups in the pre-test.

After teaching, more than 70 per cent of students in all Experimental and Baseline groups were successful in making predictions about the behaviour of electric circuits, with the differences between Experimental and Baseline groups ranging between 6 per cent and 17 per cent. Nonetheless, in all cases except for PDS and PTR, students in Experimental groups made significantly more correct predictions than those in Baseline groups. Furthermore, students in Experimental groups drew upon the taught model of electric circuits in explanations significantly more often than students in Baseline groups. It was striking that students' explanations in the three Baseline groups made use of *fewer* elements of the taught model after teaching than in the pre-test.

In order to get a sense of the difference in students' performance between the Development and Transfer Phases, we followed a similar

Table 5.3 Number of students (and percentage of class in italics) giving responses of different types following implementation of the physics teaching intervention

Phase	Case study	Pre-test (prediction) n	Correct	Incorrect	Pre-test (use of the model) n	Consistent	Incomplete	Other	Post-test (prediction) n	Correct	Incorrect	Post-test (use of the model) n	Consistent	Incomplete	Other
Development Phase	PDS	23	14.6 / *62.3*	8.3 / *37.7*	23	1.0 / *4.3*	5.0 / *21.7*	17.0 / *73.9*	23	21.2 / *92.0*	1.8 / *8.0*	23	1.0 / *4.3*	9.8 / *42.8*	12.2 / *52.9*
Development Phase	Baseline	26	20.3 / *78.2*	5.7 / *21.8*	26	4.0 / *15.4*	10.0 / *38.5*	12.0 / *46.2*	26	22.3 / *85.9*	3.7 / *14.1*	26	0.0 / *0.0*	5.5 / *21.2*	20.5 / *78.8*
Development Phase	PDD1	27	19.3 / *71.6*	7.7 / *28.4*	27	1.0 / *3.7*	12.0 / *44.4*	14.0 / *51.9*	29	25.3 / *87.3*	3.7 / *12.3*	29	4.5 / *15.5*	16.3 / *56.3*	8.2 / *28.2*
Development Phase	PDD2	28	16.7 / *59.5*	11.3 / *40.5*	28	1.0 / *3.6*	9.0 / *32.1*	18.0 / *64.3*	28	23.8 / *85.1*	4.2 / *14.9*	28	4.3 / *15.5*	10.7 / *38.1*	13.0 / *46.4*
Development Phase	Baseline	22	10.3 / *47.0*	11.7 / *53.0*	22	0.0 / *0.0*	8.0 / *36.4*	14.0 / *63.6*	20	19.0 / *95.0*	1.0 / *5.0*	20	0.2 / *0.8*	3.8 / *19.2*	16.0 / *80.0*
Development Phase	PDA	20	15.7 / *78.3*	4.3 / *21.7*	20	0.0 / *0.0*	6.0 / *30.0*	14.0 / *70.0*	20	19.7 / *98.3*	0.3 / *1.7*	20	5.7 / *28.3*	11.7 / *58.3*	2.7 / *13.3*
Development Phase	Baseline	20	17.0 / *85.0*	3.0 / *15.0*	20	0.0 / *0.0*	9.0 / *45.0*	11.0 / *55.0*	20	18.2 / *90.8*	1.8 / *9.2*	20	0.2 / *0.8*	4.8 / *24.2*	15.0 / *75.0*
Transfer Phase	PTM	28	9.3 / *33.3*	18.7 / *66.7*	28	3.0 / *10.7*	15.0 / *53.6*	10.0 / *35.7*	29	26.7 / *91.9*	2.3 / *8.1*	29	3.5 / *12.7*	14.3 / *49.4*	11.2 / *38.5*
Transfer Phase	Baseline	24	10.0 / *41.7*	14.0 / *58.3*	24	6.0 / *25.0*	11.0 / *45.8*	7.0 / *29.2*	24	18.7 / *77.8*	5.3 / *22.2*	24	0.7 / *2.8*	7.3 / *30.6*	16.0 / *66.6*
Transfer Phase	PTL	3	2.0 / *66.7*	1.0 / *33.3*	3	0.0 / *0.0*	0.0 / *0.0*	3.0 / *100*	26	23.8 / *85.3*	2.2 / *14.7*	26	1.0 / *3.9*	10.7 / *41.0*	14.4 / *55.1*
Transfer Phase	PTR	0	0 / *0*	0 / *0*	0	0	0	0	25	22.2 / *81.3*	2.8 / *18.6*	25	0.5 / *0.0*	9.5 / *40.0*	14.6 / *60.0*
Transfer Phase	PTT	25	9.0 / *36.0*	12.0 / *48.0*	25	0.0 / *0.0*	6.0 / *24.0*	19.0 / *76.0*	21	18.0 / *85.7*	3.0 / *14.3*	21	0.8 / *4.0*	6.2 / *29.4*	14.0 / *66.7*
Transfer Phase	PTK	27	13.6 / *50.6*	13.3 / *49.4*	27	1.0 / *3.7*	6.0 / *22.2*	20.0 / *74.1*	26	22.8 / *87.8*	2.7 / *12.2*	26	1.3 / *5.1*	9.0 / *34.6*	15.7 / *60.2*
Transfer Phase	Baseline	24	7.3 / *30.6*	16.6 / *69.4*	24	0.0 / *0.0*	6.0 / *25.0*	18.0 / *75.0*	23	16.4 / *71.0*	6.6 / *29.0*	23	0.0 / *0.0*	3.7 / *15.9*	19.3 / *84.1*

procedure to that used with the biology questions. We added the numbers of students whose use of the taught model of electric circuits was coded as either consistent or incomplete, and then compared the difference in the mean number in the Experimental and Baseline groups in the Development and Transfer Phases. Using this approach, students in the Experimental groups in the Development Phase were coded consistent or incomplete 43.2 per cent more often than those in Baseline groups. In the Transfer Phase, the comparable figure is 24.6 per cent. From this, we conclude that the use of the teaching interventions resulted in students achieving significantly better conceptual understanding than would have been expected had they followed the school's usual teaching approaches. However, the improvement in performance of students in classes taught by the Development Phase teachers was significantly greater than that of students in classes taught by Transfer Phase teachers.

Overview of findings about students' conceptual understandings

To what extent did students who followed the research evidence-informed biology and physics teaching interventions develop conceptual understanding consistent with the teaching goals of the interventions? Ideally all students, after teaching, would be able to make correct predictions for the diagnostic questions. Looking across both sets of data, with the exception of BTT, at least 79.9 per cent of student predictions were correct after following the designed teaching interventions, with more than 80 per cent of correct predictions in twelve out of fifteen Experimental groups.

Our aspiration is that all students' explanations, after teaching, would be consistent with the conceptual models taught. Realistically, however, it would be surprising if all students wrote explanations, for *all* questions, that drew upon *all* features of the taught conceptual models, particularly given that the diagnostic questions had an open format which provides minimal cueing about the level of detail required. Our more realistic aim, therefore, is that all students' explanations would be coded as either consistent or incomplete, with as many as possible being consistent. Students' actual results fall some considerable way short of this ideal. There are only two classes for which more than 85 per cent of students' explanations were coded as either consistent or incomplete (i.e., BDC and PDA), and in seven out of fifteen classes fewer than 50 per cent of students' explanations were coded as either consistent or incomplete.

Nevertheless, looking across our evaluations of the biology and physics teaching interventions, we can identify fifteen Experimental classes where we have Baseline data and where there is no reason to assume that students in Experimental and Baseline groups had different levels of understanding prior to teaching. In each case, students who followed the designed teaching interventions were significantly more likely to draw upon the conceptual models introduced in teaching, when compared with students in associated Baseline groups.

Consistency of implementation of the teaching sequence

So far we have presented evidence indicating that students in fifteen classes in a number of different schools achieved significantly higher learning gains, in relation to applying explanations relating to plant nutrition and electrical circuits, than students of comparable ability following the same schools' usual teaching schemes. The evidence from the input–output evaluation supports the following claim:

- Students in the fifteen classes achieved significantly higher learning gains in the relevant domains than students of comparable ability following the school's usual approach to teaching, and this is an effect of the use of the designed teaching interventions.

This claim, however, is rather limited in that it says nothing about which characteristics of the use of the teaching schemes made a difference. Although the teaching interventions are research evidence-informed, an input–output evaluation of student learning does not provide evidence about whether any research evidence-informed features of the design were actually implemented. We therefore evaluated the implementation of the designed teaching interventions by analysing video recordings of the lessons. As outlined in Chapter 4, the design of the Experimental teaching interventions involved key activities for introducing *scientific content* (following the identification of learning demands) and explicit guidance to teachers about the form of *classroom communication* to be used with these activities.

In order to judge the extent to which the way the *scientific content* was introduced was consistent with the design of the interventions, we carried out a lesson-by-lesson analysis. This involved first identifying the order in which scientific content was introduced in the published schemes for each intervention. We then analysed the video record of each lesson, and produced a lesson-by-lesson content analysis of the lessons as implemented. It was then possible to judge the extent to which the scientific content was introduced in accordance with the design intentions of the teaching intervention.

In order to judge the extent to which the teachers adopted forms of classroom communication which were consistent with the design of the interventions, we followed a similar lesson-by-lesson approach. First of all we analysed each of the lessons in the designed interventions to set out the intended movement between forms of communication (as indicated by the system of icons described in Chapter 4), as the lesson progressed. This analysis was made on a time grid on which each 'time block' of the lesson was designated as involving one of the following classes of communicative approach: non-interactive/authoritative; non-interactive/dialogic; interactive/authoritative; interactive/dialogic. In practice, this analysis was complicated somewhat by the fact that, in the schemes, the activity coded by the 'supporting' icon might involve either an interactive/authoritative or an interactive/dialogic approach. The same time grids were then used in analysing what actually happened during each lesson in relation to the forms of communication used by the teachers. This was achieved by playing the videos through, identifying major blocks of activity and deciding on the communicative approach used by the teacher for each of those blocks.

Findings about teacher implementation of the schemes

Generally speaking, teachers using the designed biology and physics teaching interventions introduced the scientific content in ways that were consistent with the design of the interventions, in both Development and Transfer Phases. In two of the case studies, although the overall presentation of scientific content followed the approach outlined in the teaching intervention, the teachers introduced additional content in response to questions raised by students. However, we did not judge that this rendered the treatment of scientific content significantly different from the design intentions of the teaching intervention. The communicative approach used by all the teachers in both the Development and Transfer Phases had some parallels with the design intentions, although there were wide variations between individual teachers.

During post-teaching interviews, both biology and physics teachers from the Development Phase of the project stated that the designed teaching interventions had addressed curriculum aims for plant nutrition and electricity better than the approach that they normally used. Furthermore, all the Development Phase teachers stated that their students had enjoyed following the designed teaching interventions, and that they themselves had also enjoyed the teaching.

Discussion and implications

This study is relatively small in scale, involving only thirteen cases where there is no evidence to challenge the validity of making comparisons between the outcomes of Experimental and Baseline teaching. Conclusions and implications need to be advanced with this in mind. Nonetheless, our findings lead us to conclude that it is possible to develop research evidence-informed teaching materials in such a way that teachers act upon many key design principles in their teaching, and that there is a significantly enhanced gain in students' learning. We noted modest but significant improvements in students' use of conceptual models after teaching, compared with those achieved by students following the schools' usual teaching programmes. This study was not designed to provide conclusive evidence about the cause of any enhanced student learning, and students' enhanced performance might in fact be caused by features of the teaching other than the design principles that informed the writing of the teaching interventions. Nonetheless, we believe that the existence of a link between the design principles of the teaching and students' performance is the most plausible explanation.

The noted improvements in students' learning followed from very short teaching interventions of a few hours, implemented by teachers for the first time. Furthermore, the Transfer Phase teachers had not been involved in the development of the teaching intervention, and were not trained in their use. Given these contextual factors, it is perhaps surprising that the learning gains were repeated across so many classes, and one is led to speculate about what might be possible if the Experimental approaches were implemented by teachers over a more extended timescale. It seems reasonable to suggest that teachers would achieve better results, in terms of their students' conceptual understanding, on the second implementation of a new teaching approach compared with the first (for example, Brown and Clement 1991). Furthermore, it seems plausible to suggest that improvements in students' conceptual understanding achieved as a result of one short teaching intervention could be built upon and augmented in subsequent teaching, particularly if a coherent approach was used throughout a school science course. For example, the gains in conceptual understanding achieved through the introduction of a charges-transferring-energy model of simple electric circuits could be built upon and extended in subsequent teaching as the concept of voltage was introduced.

Our findings pose a challenge to Matthews's (1997) claim that there is no evidence that science teaching informed by insights from 'constructivist' research on science learning is better at promoting conceptual understanding amongst students. On the contrary, they lead us to suggest that teaching arising from curriculum development focusing on the teaching of key scientific concepts, and informed by research, can indeed result in improvements to students' conceptual understanding.

The design of the biology and physics teaching interventions was informed by perspectives on classroom communication. The written teaching materials contained guidance on different kinds of teacher–student talk and their usage in science teaching, together with a system of icons to suggest the forms of teacher talk most appropriate in meeting learning aims for different teaching activities. Our evaluation of the implementation of the teaching provides some evidence that teachers in both the Development and Transfer Phases interacted with their students in ways that were broadly in line with the guidance. However, teachers' implementation of the teaching interventions did not, generally speaking, include anywhere near as much *dialogic* interaction as was intended in the design. Furthermore, in post-teaching interviews it appeared to us that some teachers were not clear about the difference between interactive/authoritative and interactive/dialogic talk (see Chapter 4). A number of teachers suggested that their lessons had involved a lot of dialogic talk because there had been a lot of question and answer work. However, in many cases this involved interactive/authoritative exchanges, heavily controlled by the teacher and with little opportunity for students to express their points of view. Much more could be done to help teachers to appreciate the difference between authoritative and dialogic talk, and to recognise the different purposes of each form of communication in science teaching. Video resources could be used productively in professional development activities to model authoritative and dialogic talk for teachers, and this would be particularly helpful if the examples used were related directly to a teaching intervention that teachers were going to use in practice. In this way, teachers' use of dialogic interactive talk around critical conceptual details (Viennot 2001) of teaching interventions might be increased.

In this study, there was no significant difference in performance on questions requiring factual recall between students who followed the designed teaching interventions and Baseline students. However, responses from students who followed the designed teaching interventions were measurably better on questions requiring the use of conceptual models to construct explanations. National assessment questions used with students aged 14 and 16 in England are often criticised by practitioners as testing factual recall rather than underlying conceptual understanding. Our findings suggest that students following the designed teaching interventions are just as capable as students following schools' normal teaching programmes in completing such questions, and were also better at answering questions requiring the use of conceptual models. Our findings lead us to believe that the use of such assessment questions may result in national assessment data overestimating students' understanding. However, we believe that there is a potentially more serious possibility. If teachers and others become used to judging students' capacity in science based upon such questions of factual recall, they may set their goals for student attainment in terms of factual recall, while failing to appreciate students' *potential* for coming to understand scientific conceptual models.

On the basis of the findings reported in this chapter, we believe that there is considerable potential for addressing the policy objective of improving students' conceptual understanding in science through curriculum development, informed by research and scholarship on teaching and learning science, together with appropriate professional development activities. The focus of professional development would be upon developing teachers' knowledge of learning demands in key science curriculum areas, developing a repertoire of classroom practices for addressing those learning demands, and recognising and becoming able to use a broader range of approaches to classroom communication for specific purposes. The primary objective of such a programme of professional development is the development of teachers' pedagogic content knowledge (PCK) (Shulman 1986).

Is it appropriate to use the evidence presented in this chapter to support a claim that science teachers who use these physics and biology teaching interventions in the future are undertaking 'research evidence-based practice'? Indeed, on the basis of the evidence presented here, should all science teachers be encouraged to use the teaching interventions set out in the two Experimental schemes? Our response to the first question is a qualified 'yes'. The evidence presented in this study shows that, for whatever reason, students who followed the designed teaching interventions as implemented by their science teachers were significantly more likely to achieve the learning aims of those teaching interventions than their peers following the school's usual approach. To this extent, in terms of the definition of research evidence-based practice presented in Chapter 1, the teaching interventions could be used in future with the justification that there is research evidence to suggest that their use is likely to lead to improvements in students' understanding of the target content.

However, we would raise several qualifications to this claim, which also bear on the second question above. The evidence produced in our study compares students' learning following the use of the teaching interventions, *in a very small sample of schools*, with what might have been achieved if they had followed the school's usual teaching. Teachers in other schools not involved in this study might therefore argue that their existing approach has features which, in principle, appear at least as well conceptualised as the designed teaching interventions. Coupled with such teachers' experience and confidence in using their existing approaches, this study provides insufficient evidence to refute the claim that using the existing teaching approach might be at least as effective as using one of the teaching schemes. A much larger trial, involving a much wider range of schools and 'normal' practices would be needed to establish more convincingly the claim that the teaching approach proposed in the designed teaching interventions should be generally adopted, or to refute it.

Furthermore, in deciding whether future implementations of the teaching interventions constitute research evidence-based practice, it is necessary to specify exactly what practice is being judged. The following claims about teaching practices might be made, and evaluated in terms of the findings of this study:

- Teachers should use the physics and biology teaching interventions in a manner consistent with their design principles.
- Teachers should use the physics and biology teaching interventions in whatever way they judge to be appropriate. (There was in fact considerable diversity in the way the teachers in the study used the teaching interventions, especially in terms of the communicative approaches used, yet significant improvements in students' performance were noted.)
- Teachers should use a teaching intervention which has the critical features of the designed ones, namely that it systematically addresses a set of research evidence-informed teaching goals, using a specified communicative approach. (The designed teaching interventions are clearly not the only way to address these research

evidence-informed teaching goals, using this communicative approach.)

The study does not provide an evidence base which could refute any of the above claims. It is not, however, possible to support the first claim, because no teacher in the sample implemented the design principles about communicative approach, particularly with regard to the use of dialogic talk. Although the data from this study supports the second and third claims, the sample size and range of 'worked examples' used in this study are not sufficient to establish either claim conclusively. This leaves a very considerable diversity in the range of practices that might be viewed as research evidence-based.

We think it is helpful to draw a distinction between *research evidence-based practice* and *appropriate practice*. As we have shown, it is entirely legitimate to justify a decision to use these teaching interventions on the grounds that there is research evidence that they 'work'. However, we also believe it is legitimate for a teacher to argue that another approach is more appropriate, possibly on the grounds that it is better matched to the needs of teachers and/or students in a particular setting, or that the improvements in understanding demonstrated by students in our study are not sufficient to justify the effort of changing an existing approach. The first of these arguments could be rendered untenable by data from a larger study. But even a larger study could not completely undermine the second argument. In other words, a judgement remains to be made about the quality and relevance of the evidence base, and the size of any effect noted, before it is sensible to make decisions about investing time and energy into changing practice. In order to claim that using one particular teaching intervention is better than a range of other practices, it is necessary to have data from a random sample of schools, as well as a range of other teaching approaches that are commonly used. The evidence provided by our study falls considerably short of this. Therefore, our answer to the question of whether science teachers should be required to use the designed teaching interventions is 'no'. However, we nonetheless believe that this study provides evidence to suggest that using the teaching interventions might well result in improvements in students' understanding of the target content. Furthermore, the fact that the design principles of the teaching interventions are explicit means that teachers are in a position to make decisions about the implementation of the teaching interventions, and possible modifications, in a principled way.

Rather than asking whether the implementation of the teaching interventions – or other educational practices – is research evidence-based or not, we think it is more helpful to ask about the nature of the evidence base on which claims rest, and the legitimate use of such evidence in informing practice. Although it *is* legitimate to argue that the use of our teaching interventions is research evidence-based practice, we prefer to think of the teaching interventions as *worked examples* (see Chapter 4). Worked examples present one way in which design principles for teaching, which are informed by research and scholarship about teaching and learning science, can be drawn upon in designing classroom teaching interventions.

An afterword: Learning from worked examples that fail to meet their goals

Our attempts to develop a worked example for the chemistry context did not meet with the same success as the other two teaching interventions, even though the same theoretical framing perspective was used. None of the Development Phase teachers used the worked example in a way which was consistent with its design principles. The teaching intervention was planned as a revision activity, because there was almost no consistency in the treatment of key chemistry content across the three schools involved in the Development Phase. By planning a revision teaching intervention to review content already taught about modelling change, we hoped that it would be possible to achieve some consistency in approach by the three teachers. However, owing to the nature of revision activities, the chemistry teaching intervention left teachers with considerable independence to make choices about which activities and examples to use with students, and how to package teaching activities into workable and motivating lessons. Although the three Development Phase teachers were very positive about its design in pre-teaching interviews, their views diverged considerably after teaching. One of the teachers modified the teaching intervention to such an extent that it is difficult to argue that his teaching was consistent with the design intentions, and in the post-teaching interview he did not feel that the teaching intervention had been successful in addressing its aims. Another of the teachers attempted to cover all the activities in the teaching intervention, rather than making selections according to her judgements of students' understanding. In the post-teaching interview she said that she had found the teaching intervention very stressful to implement. Her students responded very badly to being asked to complete diagnostic questions without formal notice and revision time, and found the teaching repetitive. Nonetheless, in the post-teaching interview the teacher stated that she had learnt a lot about her students' conceptual understanding in this area of chemistry, and the short-comings of her own school's current approach to teaching. The third chemistry teacher was very positive about the teaching intervention in the post-test interview, though the teaching as implemented deviated considerably from the design intentions.

One possible interpretation of the chemistry context is to reject the theoretical framing perspective, based on our failure to enable teachers to address the teaching goals in a way that resulted in improvements in students' learning. However, we took the view that our failure was better interpreted in terms of the design of the chemistry worked example itself. In designing the biology and physics teaching interventions, we drew upon this experience in deciding that our worked examples should be less flexible, with a view to being as clear as possible about the intended classroom practices. We spent considerable time working to package the materials into a form that we, and especially the Development Phase teachers, judged to be stimulating and workable in the classroom. We believe that this effort was critical to the success of the biology and physics teaching interventions in enabling the teachers to conduct motivating lessons that were broadly consistent with the design intentions of the teaching, and that resulted in students achieving improved conceptual understanding.

The contrast between how the chemistry, and biology and physics teaching interventions were received and used provides a stark illus-tration of the difficulties involved in drawing upon research findings to inform practice. Our study shows that the process of developing classroom practices for teaching scientific concepts requires at least as much intellectual and developmental work as the process of generating knowledge about teaching and learning science.

Summary

In this chapter we have described how we evaluated the effectiveness of research evidence-informed teaching interventions in meeting stated objectives for students' conceptual understanding. We have shown that it is possible to develop research evidence-informed teaching materials in such a way that teachers act in accordance with many of the key design principles in their teaching, and that there was a significantly enhanced gain in students' learning. We then discussed the significance of this evidence for future practice in science teaching. Although the two interventions described in this chapter meet our definition of research evidence-based practice, we do not think that the evidence is sufficient to justify advocating that everyone should use the teaching interventions. Rather, we suggest that the study presents evidence for cautious optimism that the practice of science teaching can be improved through research evidence-informed curriculum development of the kind undertaken, and that teachers should therefore review their current teaching approach for these topics and ideas in the light of these findings.

Chapter 6

Using designed teaching materials to stimulate changes in practice

The previous two chapters (Chapters 4 and 5) have discussed and explored the implications and outcomes of following what might be thought the most obvious and direct method of increasing the influence of research on teaching: designing teaching interventions in the light of research findings, and then evaluating the outcomes when these are implemented to obtain the kind of evidence that might warrant recommending others to adopt these interventions. These chapters have highlighted the potential, and the challenges for both developers and researchers, of such an approach.

This chapter explores a rather less direct strategy for increasing the influence of research on teachers' actions and decisions in planning and delivering lessons. The central idea was to provide teachers, not with research *findings*, or with a teaching sequence informed by these, but with *instruments* based upon those used by researchers to probe learners' ideas and understandings, in the form of a bank of diagnostic questions that they could use in their own teaching. These would make it easier for teachers to collect data to monitor students' understandings and misunderstandings in the normal course of teaching, and this in turn might inform their subsequent actions and choices.

Introduction

There were several reasons for choosing the strategy of giving teachers research tools rather than summaries of research findings. First, it may

Authored by Robin Millar and Vicky Hames

help to circumvent a common practitioner response to reported research findings – that the students involved or the teaching context must be different from their own, so the results reported would not apply to them (for some examples of this, see Chapter 8). By using diagnostic questions, teachers would collect data on their own students, which would be clearly relevant to their decision making. Second, the publication of diagnostic tests based on research, and data collected by using them, has been strikingly effective in stimulating change in college physics teaching in the US (Hestenes *et al.* 1992; Mazur 1997; Redish 2003). Teachers using them have become dissatisfied with the outcomes of their teaching and have made changes to try to improve student learning. The provision of good diagnostic tools might stimulate similar reflection and change at school level. Third, the work of Black and Wiliam (1998a, 1998b) on formative assessment suggests that its systematic use can lead to significant learning gains. A critical factor for the wider adoption of formative assessment practices, and for their quality, may be the availability of good assessment questions. Providing a supply of good diagnostic questions makes it significantly easier for teachers to change their practice in this way.

We will return at the end of this chapter to consider further how this strategy and its outcomes relate to the characterisations of research evidence-informed practice and research evidence-based practice in Chapter 1.

The research study

The aim of this part of the EPSE work, then, was to explore the extent to which teachers' practices might be changed, in ways which take account of the findings of research on students' learning, by providing them with a bank of diagnostic questions based on research. The first, and very substantial, phase of the work was the development of diagnostic question banks. The way in which this was done has already been described in Chapter 3. As explained there, the development was carried out in collaboration with a small group of teachers and LEA science advisers, who chose science topics on which to work and assisted in the selection, modification and pilot testing of diagnostic questions. The outcome was three large banks of diagnostic questions, on electric circuits, particle models of matter, and forces and motion, totalling over 500 items. Some examples are shown in Chapter 3 (Figures 3.1–3.4).

As compared to research evidence-informed teaching interventions, like those discussed in Chapters 4 and 5, these diagnostic question banks can be used more flexibly. Each contains more questions than any teacher would be likely to use – so choice and selection are required. The question banks were, however, carefully organised in the light of a detailed analysis of the content of each science domain. They therefore suggest a pathway through the main ideas that have to be mastered in coming to a fuller understanding of the domain – and this, in turn, may influence the order in which teachers using the banks tackle these topics.

Teachers in ten schools (eight secondary; two primary) were given a bank of diagnostic questions on one science topic, with some very general suggestions about possible ways of using them. Four had helped in developing the banks; the others had heard of the project through local or regional teacher networks and had enquired about getting involved. All were therefore volunteers. In most schools, the materials were used by several teachers in the science department. We then monitored, over a school year, how these teachers chose to use the question bank with their classes, their views on it, and the evidence of changes in classroom practices and students' responses. This was done mainly through extended interviews, with written questionnaires to collect additional information. It resulted in sixteen case studies of teachers' use of these diagnostic question banks, with additional data from a further seven teachers. The schools involved were all local education authority primaries or comprehensives, of a range of sizes and locations (city, suburban, small town). The teachers (thirteen male, ten female) included biology, chemistry and physics specialists, with teaching experience ranging from one year to over twenty-five years. Whilst the sample of schools and teachers was small, it was not in any obvious way atypical or unrepresentative of schools and science teachers in England more generally. In the extracts which follow, secondary teachers are identified as T, and primary teachers as PT, followed by a number.

How teachers used the diagnostic question banks

Not surprisingly, several teachers' initial perception of the diagnostic question banks was as a source of items for making up tests. As one put it:

> I thought, oh good, questions, because we're so short of useful questions. And . . . it takes a long time to develop good questions. . . . We needed a new test because of the changes in the scheme of work . . . so I looked in the pack and chose the questions that

seemed to correspond to our scheme of work, and just pulled a selection out.

(T1)

Another described how her ideas about using the question bank changed as she looked at it more closely and began using some questions:

I flicked through them and thought, oh yeah, they look like tests, you know, tons of it. And then when you look at it, you think, oh, no, no. And they were so interesting to use. The use for me is opening up the discussion, thinking about how they're actually perceiving things, that was the interesting bit.

(T11)

Only a few teachers reported using a selection of questions as a formal pre-test before beginning a new topic. More favoured a less formal means of checking students' understanding. This typically involved a short whole-class discussion, focused by one or two questions selected by the teacher, presented on an overhead projector. For one teacher, this was her principal way of using the diagnostic questions:

For starts and ends, that's been my principal use. . . . at the start of a lesson, basically testing the ideas taught the previous lesson. You know, testing what I've taught them the lesson before. Often that's how I'll start the next lesson. Have they got it? And sometimes at the end of a lesson.

(T4)

Perhaps more surprisingly, more than half of the teachers reported using diagnostic questions as stimulus material for small-group discussion, and many talked more about this than about any other use. Various ways of organising these discussions were reported:

I put them in groups of two . . . and I asked them . . . to look at the questions, read them carefully and then try to find the appropriate answers. I gave maybe initially about five minutes on each. And then I asked around the room for their answers . . . and when we'd been round the room discussing these, then I clarified what I thought the question was after, and then they turned on to the next page.

(T1)

> I photocopied the questions in little booklets and got them to discuss in pairs and then [put pairs together] in a four.
>
> (T3)

> I asked them to do the questions individually. And then I put them into groups of four and I said 'I want you to compare your answers. If you agree, fine, if you don't, then I want you to sort out between the four of you what you think the right answer is.' And we did that in batches of, I don't know, half a dozen questions. . . . I then asked different groups to tell the other groups what they thought the right answer was. And we had a whole-class discussion about what the right answer was.
>
> (T10)

One teacher explained his decision to use questions as group, rather than individual, tasks in terms of the higher levels of student participation that resulted:

> Together, as a group, they often put forward ideas from their group. Because that's not me, that's our group saying this, so there's less fear in it. I mean, some have no problem, they'll just say what they want. But this group thing helps, because it's 'we think', not 'I think'.
>
> (T7)

Changes in teachers' practices

The aim, in providing teachers with a bank of research-informed diagnostic questions, was to stimulate changes in their practices. So to what extent did the provision of these diagnostic assessment resources lead to changes in practice? And to what kinds of changes? Several teachers indicated that students' answers to diagnostic questions had made them re-think their teaching plans. For example, one primary teacher was surprised that many of her students gave wrong answers to one particular question about the effect of opening a switch in a series electric circuit:

> It's easy to take for granted that by that age the children have got a fairly good idea of the complete circuit. But I found there was one question in particular, that quite a significant number of children got wrong. . . . What it showed me was . . . that I still needed to consolidate the work on the complete circuit, which surprised me slightly.
>
> (PT2)

A secondary teacher (T11) similarly reported her surprise at students' answers to a question about classifying events as physical or chemical change, and saying whether 'new substances' are formed, describing their responses to questions that she judged 'easy' as 'rubbish . . . absolute nonsense'. Even where students' answers confirmed a teacher's view that a particular idea was difficult, the clarity of the evidence of students' learning difficulties made it more likely to cause a change of plan:

> It confirmed the areas that I knew they struggled with. But I think it sort of made me more aware, you know. Perhaps I thought they had understood it through my teaching. And it made me actually more aware that, no, I had to stop and revisit certain areas. . . . It made it very clear that the students hadn't understood where perhaps I thought they had, and I was moving on. So it was very good in that respect.
>
> (T16)

Conversely, one teacher found that his class understood speed–time graphs better than he expected and concluded that 'perhaps with some of these groups, I should push it along a bit quicker' (T9).

As regards teaching approaches, some teachers did not feel that using the diagnostic questions had greatly altered how they taught. Asked directly about this, one replied:

> Not really because . . . I've known for years that misconception's there, so I always address it. . . . This was just a way of doing it. . . . I've been teaching the topic for so long now, you tend to register the things that they commonly misunderstand or get wrong. So I've had some means of attacking those things. These are the quickest and best way I've ever seen of doing it.
>
> (T4)

Later in the same interview, however, he did acknowledge that using the questions had altered the way he taught:

> Oh it has [influenced my own teaching style], without question, in a beneficial way. . . . I mean if I was the sort of teacher that was always prompting discussion then it probably wouldn't have been a necessity, I wouldn't have needed that. But I did need that and

it's helped, without question, it's helped. I'm having more discussions in class than previously, which is a good thing.

(T4)

Others made similar comments, about increased use of discussion in their classes, and about the quality of that discussion. Several attributed this to the multiple-choice format of many of the diagnostic questions:

I think that's a very useful feature of them, the fact that they do give alternatives, so the kids aren't thinking in a vacuum. They do actually have a starting point.

(T10)

It made a lot more openings for discussion. Whereas sometimes with other questions and other ideas, you tend to get limited with what kind of alleys you can go down. . . . With those, because . . . the children had . . . lots of ideas in front of them, I thought that it was better. . . . They've got ideas already and then they can bring their own in with it.

(T13)

Several linked this to a general value that many of the teachers seemed to share, that 'good teaching' involves developing ideas through dialogue, with active student involvement and participation, rather than 'transmission' of ideas from teacher to student. In contrast to this, research evidence suggests that science classroom talk is often teacher-centred, and authoritative rather than dialogic – and that the lack of opportunity to express and explore ideas and understandings in their own words impedes student learning (Lemke 1990; Mortimer and Scott 2003). The reason may lie, however, in teachers' difficulty in seeing *how* to make lessons more dialogic than in any unwillingness to do so. And this difficulty may be greatest where teachers are working in topics with which they are less familiar, or where they feel less confident and secure in their own knowledge. For example, a chemistry graduate in her first year of teaching explained how a diagnostic question bank had helped her to move from 'giving' students the key ideas to enabling these to 'emerge' more gradually:

I'm not very experienced and, especially with forces and things, when I bring it together at the end, or when I'm trying to bring it in – the fact when you have the force opposing motion, what would happen to the speed and so on – I tend to find that I more or less give it to them in a way, because trying to get them to discuss it, to bring it in, I find it quite hard. Whereas . . . I was able to do the diagrams on the board and they came up and did the forces and arrows and things. . . . We came to it together, which is a lot better. I thought like I'd actually done proper teaching then.

(T13)

This is not only an issue for beginning teachers. A Head of Chemistry with several years' teaching experience talked similarly about how the diagnostic question bank on forces and motion had helped her teach the topic differently, and in a manner she found more satisfying:

I'm not a traditional teacher in my approach. It's not my style of teaching. But I've probably stuck a bit more to that in physics because of not being as confident in the subject. Whereas this has forced me to take a different approach . . . much more the approach that I would take with chemistry . . . much more open, you know, rather than me just giving information and working through things, a much more sort of interactive, discursive approach, which is a style of teaching I prefer. I think it's a better way of going about things, but perhaps I haven't been as confident in physics before to risk it. . . . I come up with ideas myself for biology and chemistry, but I find it much more difficult to come up with them for the physics area. So yes, for me, it's given me material that I can build things around and have confidence in them working. Which has been nice, because, like I say, it is an area that I find it quite difficult to be imaginative about.

(T15)

So provision of diagnostic questions may be particularly helpful to teachers teaching outside their own science subject specialism. Previous studies (Hacker and Rowe 1985; Harlen and Holroyd 1997) have shown that many teachers fall back on a transmission model of teaching when working in areas in which they lack confidence and breadth of understanding. A diagnostic question bank highlights key points, and suggests the order in which these should be taught, as well as providing ideas for lesson activities that encourage student participation and dialogue.

Several teachers also indicated how the diagnostic question banks had helped them, and their school colleagues, to improve their own understanding of the science topics covered. In one school, all science staff wrote individual answers to a set of diagnostic questions and then discussed these together. Reflecting on this experience, one commented:

> I think my understanding of the topic has improved as a result of going through the questions. . . . And I think that, consequently, I will become better at dealing with it in the future, at whatever level it happens to be. Because I think, you know, even science teachers have the same misconceptions. . . . I had a misconception with forces, that I never knew I had. . . . And a lot of us had at least one misconception. And when you start addressing that yourself, you start getting more confident.
>
> (T15)

Another teacher in the same department regarded this as 'the best piece of INSET I've had in years' (T2). A few teachers also commented on the teaching of points within their specialism. For example, one physics teacher thought that questions on identifying forces had made his students analyse situations more precisely than before:

> T1: With these questions, you've got to actually understand more of what the mechanism is which leads to the forces arising in physical situations. . . . the questions . . . encouraged them to say, well, there's something happening at this point which means there must be a force acting at that point in that direction and also a force acting at that point in that direction . . . and one's bigger than the other or whatever, you know. And I don't think that had ever been examined in detail in any exams that I've seen. And so we needed to discuss that.
>
> I: Do you think that has changed how you teach the topic?
>
> T1: Yes, definitely. I think that's quite a significant difference, as well.

In another example, a very experienced physics teacher reflected on how a discussion, in a class of 15-year-olds, of some questions about the motion of objects set in motion by a kick or throw, made him aware of the value of the concept of 'momentum' in supporting students' thinking:

> Although momentum isn't on the syllabus, during the discussion it was perfectly obvious that we needed some sort of word to describe the property of a moving body, independent of the forces on it. So

we just invented the word 'momentum' as a way of talking about things . . . it came out of the discussion, it became necessary in the discussion to use momentum. . . . But once we got that idea introduced, as soon as we looked at this one, kids who would have normally said, 'well it's moving up, so there must be a force upwards', immediately said 'no, no, no, there's only one force and that's a downward force and that's why it slows down'. So I felt that they had managed to [grasp something important].

(T10)

These might be seen as examples of changes in the teacher's pedagogical content knowledge (Shulman 1987), stimulated by their use of these diagnostic question banks.

Impact on student learning

Changing teachers' practices is not an end in itself, but a means towards the end of improving students' understanding or enjoyment of the subject. In an exploratory study such as this, however, it was not possible to obtain 'hard' evidence of improvements in learning. Teachers used the materials in different ways, whilst following quite different teaching schemes. Outcome measures differed from school to school, and changing these was often not within the control of the teacher (and certainly not of the researchers). When asked directly about student learning in the topic areas covered by the question banks, teachers invariably said that this had been improved:

Much better [than before]. They understood a lot better, this Year 9, so that was brilliant. . . . The marks were very good . . . apart from an odd one or two. . . . Everybody was able to understand much, much easier, and was able to answer those questions.

(T5)

Several also pointed to changes in the quality of learning:

I think they took it more on board, because they had to discuss it, and they had to back up their answers, and they had to say why they thought it. . . . I felt quite confident they'd got it and they knew why. It wasn't just a case of just reeling it off and writing the right answer, you know, because they've actually thought about it.

(T13)

Another felt that changes in the way she had taught the topic had led to better learning by the less able students in the group. As the new approach had been more enjoyable for the able students, they had also gained from it:

> The less able students in the group were forced to think about it when perhaps they would otherwise have just written notes. . . . The fact that we had discussions going meant that that happened. My feelings are that certainly the less able in the group were much better informed about the topic at the end of the process than they were at the beginning . . . based on the evidence of the questions that they've answered, and now looking at the past SATs questions that we're looking at, topics that are related, how they're answering those now, and they're doing a better job of them. I think the more able students in the group enjoyed it, probably would have got it anyway, but enjoyed it. And therefore, that was as useful as anything, you know.
>
> (T15)

Several teachers also questioned the value of summative tests for measuring students' learning. One who had used some diagnostic questions *during* her teaching of a topic chose not to add any to the end-of-topic test because 'by using them the way I did, I'd found out what I needed to know' (PT2). Other teachers' comments echoed this sense of gaining more valid insights from conversations and discussions during the teaching:

> I actually felt I'd got more of an idea going round and eaves-dropping on their conversations than I did with their written comments. The written comments were of some use, but I think it was the discussion and listening to that that I found more useful.
>
> (T3)

> The way you get at kids' thinking is to talk to them about it, I think. And get them to talk about it.
>
> (T10)

Promoting research evidence-informed practice

The aim of this study was to explore the extent to which science teachers' practice might be changed by providing them with a specific resource – a bank of diagnostic questions based on probes used in research on learning, which embody insights and findings of this research. Teachers' practice might, as a result, become more research evidence-informed (as characterised in Figure 1.1) in two senses. First, it might take more note of learning difficulties identified by research. Second, teachers' decisions might be more systematically informed by evidence that they had themselves collected of their students' learning.

So did this approach work, and what can we learn from it about the uptake of research evidence-informed teaching materials and the effects of this on practice? Given the relatively small scale of the study, and the self-selected group of teachers involved, any answers must necessarily be tentative. Nonetheless, these case studies provided encouraging evidence that teachers' practices can be significantly influenced by carefully designed teaching materials. The diagnostic questions helped teachers to identify more precisely the key ideas that are crucial for developing understanding of these science topics, and to focus their teaching more strongly on these. In the words of one teacher, 'they remind you of what you should be doing, when there are so many other things that can distract you' (T12). Significantly, most of the group independently reported an increase in the amount of discussion in their classes, focused on key ideas and often sustained for extended periods of time, even in lower ability sets. Many also saw these discussions as ideal opportunities for monitoring the development of individual students' understanding. Several teachers also indicated that the diagnostic question banks helped them to teach outside their specialist area in more interactive ways, and with a clearer understanding of the key ideas to emphasise and the order in which to teach them.

It does not, of course, follow that *any* teaching materials based on research would similarly influence teachers' practices. It was clear that these teachers made judgements about the qualities of *these* materials, in terms both of their presentation and (more importantly) of their 'fit' to their teaching situation and the challenges they currently face. Indeed teachers' initial reactions to a diagnostic question bank were invariably based on their judgement of its usefulness as teaching material, rather than on the fact that it was (or claimed to be) 'based on research'. Fullan (1991) identifies 'quality and practicality' of a new approach as key determinants of its uptake, and hence of its capacity to stimulate change. Similarly, Doyle and Ponder (1977–8) suggest that new materials and approaches must pass the test of teachers' 'practicality ethic' to be taken up, that is, they must be seen to be relevant to their needs, and to fit their situation and context, and it must be clear how they should be used. These diagnostic materials were clearly seen by these teachers to meet these criteria. First, they fitted well with other current initiatives. Almost all of the teachers involved saw the EPSE diagnostic questions as a way of implementing 'assessment for learning', one of the principal targets of the National Strategy for Key Stage 3 (age 11–14) in England (DfES 2002). Several contrasted the specific and practical support that the question banks provided favourably with the generic in-service sessions they had experienced. The use of a diagnostic question to start or end a lesson was seen by several as a way of responding to the pressure, again from the Key Stage 3 National Strategy but also reinforced by school inspection practices, for three-part lessons with a whole-class 'plenary' at the beginning and end. Second, the diagnostic question banks had a low 'entry threshold': they could be introduced initially in relatively small ways, to 'test the water', without great risk or time commitment. Third, they were seen as a 'flexible' resource. As one teacher put it:

> It fitted in with my own teaching. . . . I thought I can use those in a similar way to what I would teach anyway. It was just like adding to it rather than altering what I was going to do completely.
>
> (T3)

Another remarked similarly:

> You have things that fit with you, don't you, as a person. There were some things I looked at and thought, yes, I do that already. And some things I looked at and I thought, oh yes, I would like to do that now. It's still me, but it's something I haven't done before. So, yes, I like that sheet. I like that approach. I'll have a go at that.
>
> (T6)

Compared to a fully worked-out teaching intervention, these diagnostic question banks left many choices and decisions to the teacher. Specific questions could be chosen to fit the current needs of students, schemes of work and syllabuses. Indeed the banks deliberately included more questions on many topics than teachers could possibly use, so some selection and choice were essential. Flexibility, however, carries with it a risk – of relatively minor and superficial change. Huberman (1993) uses the term 'bricolage' to characterise the way that teachers change and develop their practice. Like artisans, they pick up and use materials or techniques that fit their own style and intentions. Thompson and Zeuli (1999) comment that 'This kind of craftsmanly tinkering is quite practical and eminently sensible, but it is also quite conservative' (p. 350). Changing practice through the provision of teaching materials involves striking a balance between being too similar to current practice (and so not effecting any real change) and too different (and not adopted). In this respect, diagnostic questions are a kind of Trojan Horse: their form looks familiar and they fit easily with current practice, so they are taken up; but they then challenge that practice through the data they generate. And they can also subtly shape practice through their emphases, and the teaching sequence they imply.

We might also ask: what *kinds* of change are we trying to achieve by providing these materials? Writing about teachers' continuing professional development (CPD), another type of intervention designed to promote change in practice, Harland and Kinder (1997) identify a range of different kinds of intended outcome. Of these, the easiest to achieve are 'material and provisionary' outcomes – where the aim is to make new materials available to the teacher. At the other end of the spectrum, they place 'value congruence' outcomes – where the aim is a change in the teacher's values to align them more closely with those implicit in a new approach. At first sight, the adoption of a more interactive and discursive teaching style, in which assessment is an integral part of teaching and where the pace and sequence of instruction is modified in the light of feedback, might appear to require a considerable value shift for many teachers and so be difficult to achieve. Yet many teachers appeared to be willing to adopt at least some aspects of these approaches. Our interpretation of this is that using the diagnostic materials, in the way they did, did not require these teachers to question or alter their values, but rather helped them to teach in ways that were more closely in line with those values, when teaching science topics where they had previously found this difficult. Prompting more class discussions was described as 'good'; teaching ideas about forces in a more dialogic manner felt like 'proper teaching'; it enabled teachers to adopt 'a better way of going about things' when teaching material they were less confident about.

The strategy which this study adopted merges two distinct perspectives on the research–practice interface: a *research-into-practice* view (which aims to increase the use by teachers of research done by others) and an *action research* view (which encourages teachers to research their own practice in order to improve it). We were encouraging these teachers to collect evidence of their students' learning in order to stimulate change, by providing tools whose origins lay in previous research, to shape this process. This led, in many cases, to an increased emphasis on key ideas, and to changes in the pace of instruction and, perhaps most strikingly, in the nature of classroom interaction. As these changes are a direct response to research evidence of learning difficulties, and their teaching schemes more closely followed research-informed analyses of content, these teachers' practice can clearly be said to have become more research evidence-informed as a result of having access to these diagnostic question banks.

Towards research evidence-based practice

Finally, we might ask: how far can the approach adopted in this study be said to promote more research evidence-based practice, as we have characterised it in Chapter 1? The focus here is on outcomes, rather than on the design of teaching materials – on research evidence that the approach leads to better learning outcomes. As we have acknowledged above, this study on its own provides no strong warrant for such a claim. The variety of teaching programmes in use in schools, leading to wide variation in the ways that teachers used a flexible resource such as these diagnostic question banks, made it impossible to design and implement an experimental evaluation. Case studies provide rather weaker evidence of outcome. However, the high proportion of the teachers involved in this study who independently reported, and provided examples of, a striking increase in use of student–student discussion in their classes suggests that this outcome might also be expected in a larger study. At the very least, we would see our study as having identified this as a plausible hypothesis that is worth testing more rigorously.

This, it might be argued, is an outcome in terms of teachers' practices rather than student learning outcomes. But if the effectiveness of certain general approaches has been established by previous research, then perhaps the role of more specific and focused research should not be to re-establish these but rather to provide evidence of how they might be facilitated and used more widely. For example, an extensive body of research points to the critical importance of language use by learners, to establish and extend their understanding of abstract ideas and concepts (Barnes 1976; Mercer and Wegerif 1998; Mercer 2000). If we accept that teaching of such ideas which involves classroom dialogue and opportunities for structured discussion, rather than consisting entirely of teacher-focused 'transmission' teaching, is more effective, then further research to re-discover that this is so is redundant. The more important task is to try to understand the barriers to the wider influence of this research finding. If, as would appear from some of the teachers' comments reported above, lack of ideas and materials rather than lack of will is a critical factor, then research that explores effective ways of providing these is central to facilitating practices which are research evidence-based.

To take a second example, directly related to our work, the review of research on formative assessment by Black and Wiliam (1998a) provides evidence that the use of formative assessment methods leads to better student learning. Rather than seeking to add to the evidence that this is so, a more pertinent research objective might be to understand better the obstacles and barriers to its wider use. The comments of teachers involved in this study, that they could monitor changes and developments in individual students' ideas and understandings, by observing their responses to diagnostic questions and tasks in the classroom situation, suggest that suitably structured teaching materials can facilitate – indeed may even be essential in enabling – the use of formative assessment.

The intervention of providing these diagnostic banks for teachers to use therefore facilitated and encouraged practices that are not only more strongly research evidence-informed, but whose general effectiveness has been warranted by research – and which are, therefore, also research evidence-based.

Summary

Providing teachers with banks of diagnostic questions resulted in changes in their teaching practices. Few used them primarily as test items. Instead many used the questions to review key points with the class at the beginning or end of a lesson, and to stimulate discussion in small groups. Teachers reported sustained and focused discussions involving groups of a wide range of ability. Many found the questions a valuable resource in helping them to identify key teaching points, putting these in a developmental sequence, and

continued

teaching them in a more interactive way. This was particularly so for teachers working outside their specialist science area, or in the early years of their teaching career. Most were also convinced that their students' learning had been enhanced as a result of these changes in their teaching practices.

Chapter 7

Teaching 'ideas about science'

The role of research in improving practice

Chapter 2 discussed the role of research in curriculum planning at the macro-level, looking at the extent of expert agreement about what students should be taught 'about science'. This chapter looks at what is involved in developing teachers' practices in teaching the themes that emerged as priorities in the Delphi study outlined there. Although this chapter focuses on the teaching of one specific aspect of the science curriculum, the messages are relevant to curricular initiatives in other subjects, particularly those which involve reflection on the nature of knowledge in the subject, or the forms of enquiry and reasoning used. The chapter documents the challenges faced by teachers in teaching 'ideas about science' explicitly, considering the design of lessons (the 'intended curriculum'), their implementation in classrooms (the 'implemented curriculum'), and the students' learning outcomes (the 'attained curriculum').

Background – the basis for development

What is there to guide the development of the intended curriculum in the complex area of 'ideas about science' and what factors will affect the implemented and attained curriculum? We use the term 'ideas about science' to describe an area of the curriculum comprising the nature of scientific knowledge, the methods of scientific enquiry, and the institutions and social practices of science. Although these aspects, particularly methods of scientific enquiry, have traditionally been an implicit part of the science curriculum, the major emphasis has been on

Authored by Mary Ratcliffe, Jonathan Osborne and Hannah Bartholomew

the canon of consensual scientific knowledge, rather than its epistemological underpinnings – a focus on 'what we know' rather than 'how we know'. This focus is also reflected in the nature of high-stakes assessment, such as national examinations, which have a significant 'backwash' effect on teaching (Harlen *et al.* 1994). Teachers tend to shape their practices to reflect assessment priorities and prepare students for the particular forms of high-stakes assessment questions which they will experience.

With a lack of tradition in assessing 'ideas about science' in public examinations, there is little to encourage teachers to give 'ideas about science' prominence or to guide them in teaching. This is in sharp contrast to domains of scientific knowledge such as those discussed in Chapters 3–6, where a long history of teaching, and therefore an extensive professional knowledge base, exists. There is thus far more limited professional understanding of what it means to teach 'ideas about science' explicitly, a limited resource base of teaching materials, and little expertise in assessing outcomes.

The themes from the Delphi study described in Chapter 2 provide much needed evidence of which 'ideas about science' should be addressed in the formal science curriculum up to the age of 16. However, each of these themes (Chapter 2, Table 2.1) needs contextualisation within a scientific domain. Put simply, it is difficult to see how any of the 'ideas about science' themes could be taught or learnt in the abstract, without exemplification through particular scientific content. Thus, in determining teaching strategies and materials, not only do we need to consider how to develop a particular 'idea about science' explicitly but also the most appropriate contexts in which to do this. In using a piece of consensual scientific knowledge ('what we know') for teaching an 'idea about science' ('how we know'), however, there may be conflicts for teachers and learners. For instance, normally in teaching established scientific knowledge, teachers tend to renegotiate classroom observations and events to achieve a social consensus (Atkinson and Delamont 1977), and persuade their pupils of the validity of the scientific world-view (Ogborn *et al.* 1996). In contrast, teaching for epistemological understanding requires knowledge claims to be opened up to scrutiny, with competing evidence and explanations being challenged and explored, often using language which is interpretative and figurative (Sutton 1995). In shifting the balance of the science curriculum to pay more *explicit* attention to 'ideas about science', we may be asking students (and teachers) to hold simultaneously two rather different views about the purposes of science lessons – one as a means for conveying understanding of established scientific knowledge, another as an exploration of knowledge claims. Preparing to teach 'ideas about science' is therefore not straightforward.

It is perhaps not surprising then that much previous research has focused on exploring teachers' and students' understanding of important 'ideas about science'. Many of the studies exploring teachers' conceptions of the nature of science have shown that many teachers' views tend towards the naïve (Kouladis and Ogborn 1989; Lederman 1992; Abd-El-Khalick and Lederman 2000). A lack of refined understanding is unsurprising given that teachers are themselves a product of a traditional science education where any comprehension of 'ideas about science' was developed implicitly, if at all (Gallagher 1991; Lakin and Wellington 1994; Mellado 1998). Whilst it might be supposed that teachers' understanding of 'ideas about science' directly affects the way in which they present science to students, the relationship is, however, complex. Several studies have shown that curriculum imperatives are perhaps the dominant imperatives which determine the nature of science presented in the classroom rather than teachers' philosophical stances (Duschl and Wright 1989; Brickhouse 1991; Hodson 1993). The implication is that if the curriculum and its assessment are changed, teachers will adapt their practice to address this domain more explicitly.

Research on students' understanding of 'ideas about science' has similarly concentrated on documenting the conceptions students have, showing likewise their often limited and naïve views (Lederman and O'Malley 1990; Désautels and Larochelle 1998). Such research has largely been conducted outside the classroom, using interviews (Driver *et al.* 1996) or written instruments (Aikenhead 1987; Norris and Phillips 1994) to elicit and capture students' understanding. Written instruments have focused on revealing students' conceptions of major themes rather than 'measuring' the achievement of specific learning outcomes. There are just a few examples (for example, Enger and Yager 1998, 2001) to guide the construction of valid and reliable tools for assessing specific learning outcomes in relation to 'ideas about science' – something which is of concern when clarity in assessment is an important feature in specifying the 'attained' curriculum.

Very little research has focused on activities in the classroom, exploring either the nature of students' learning through focused teaching or the development and evaluation of targeted interventions (the 'implemented' curriculum). Exploratory studies involving teaching interventions and raising the issue of appropriate pedagogic styles (for example, Leach *et al.* 2003; Brickhouse *et al.* 2000) have indicated students' lack of appreciation that the focus of learning was on the nature of science rather than on science content, and the lack of confidence of teachers in adapting their practice to include such teaching. In summary, there is a limited professional knowledge and research base to inform both the assessment of specific learning goals (the 'attained' curriculum) and the construction of appropriate teaching interventions (the 'implemented' curriculum).

Challenges in research design

In developing this study, we had to consider the paucity of existing evidence and professional expertise in deciding how best to use the available resources. In working towards research evidence-based practice, a teaching intervention worth testing needs to have specific learning outcomes and valid and reliable means of measuring them. We could thus have focused on the development of valid and reliable instruments to evaluate some specific learning outcomes, along the lines of the work described in Chapter 3. There was also a need, however, to develop teaching interventions which recognised the challenges to teachers in changing their practice, given the unfamiliarity of explicit teaching of 'ideas about science'. We considered that this latter issue was a priority. A teaching intervention has to be professionally plausible to teachers, regardless of any research provenance. We thus worked with practising teachers as they developed lessons to target specific learning goals resulting from consideration of the nine 'ideas about science' themes identified by the Delphi study reported in Chapter 2. This approach enabled the identification of the barriers and opportunities for students' learning in specific science lessons.

Before knowing the outcomes of the Delphi study, our original aim had been to develop and evaluate teaching materials to improve students' attainment of identified learning targets, operating within the constraints of the current science curriculum in England. Given the nature of the themes that emerged from the Delphi study, it proved too large a task to develop valid and reliable outcome measures for all specific learning targets relevant to the themes. Despite the difficulties in measuring learning outcomes in the general area of 'ideas about science', however, we still wanted to explore students' understanding of some key aspects of the nature of science and try to identify any changes resulting from their experience of explicit teaching of themes identified by the Delphi study.

Figure 7.1 summarises the research design envisaged, showing the intended parallel activities – development work with teachers in

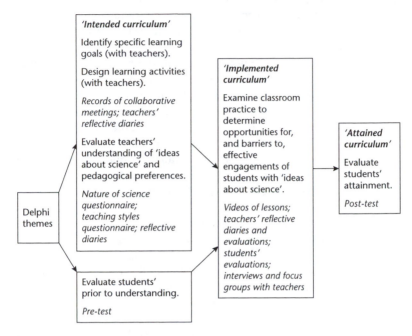

Figure 7.1   Research design and data collection methods

translating curriculum intentions into lessons with specific learning goals and evaluation of the resulting implementation; and development of assessment items to measure students' learning with respect to some aspects of the nine themes from the Delphi study.

Teachers' practices in developing and teaching focused lessons on 'ideas about science'

We recruited eleven teachers: three primary (a fourth recruit dropped out at an early stage because of pressure of work), four lower secondary and four upper secondary. We worked with them to see whether and how the nine 'ideas about science' themes from the Delphi study could become an integral part of their teaching, how learning goals could be operationalised and how student achievement evaluated. In recruiting the secondary school teachers we aimed for a balance across type of school (single-sex/mixed; comprehensive/selective) and background in main subject discipline (biology/chemistry/physics). Recruits were volunteers – experienced teachers who were interested in the project but whose understanding and practice in teaching the nature of science were unknown at the outset.

Although teachers were not selected on the basis of their level of understanding of 'ideas about science', we considered it useful to have background data on their knowledge and on their pedagogic preferences. Outcomes from administration of a previously validated questionnaire (Cotham 1979) indicated that, on most aspects of the nature of science, the eleven teachers were showing 'indeterminate' views. Thus these teachers were not atypical in presenting fairly unsophisticated, but not totally naïve, views of the nature of science which other researchers have shown to be prevalent (Abd-El-Khalick and Lederman 2000).

Four initial one-day meetings allowed collaboration between researchers and teachers in: examining the pedagogical implications of the themes; developing lessons addressing the themes; and considering methods of evaluating the student learning outcomes. Teachers felt that specific learning goals relevant to a theme could generally be tackled in a single lesson. The teachers undertook to teach at least eight lessons over a period of two terms to a target class, addressing as many of the nine themes as they could. Two further one-day meetings explored the outcomes for teachers and students in addressing 'ideas about science' explicitly in lessons. We used a range of data-collection methods from which evaluations of teachers' practice in planning and teaching could be made (shown in italics in Figure 7.1).

One of the first steps in discussing the aims of the project with teachers was to present the nine themes of 'ideas about science' arising from the Delphi study and encourage them to examine the extent to which they were already addressing these in their teaching. The first reaction for many teachers was to assert that these themes were part of the curriculum and that they were addressing them implicitly through students' engagement in practical work and investigations. However, further discussion as to what the themes really meant when translated into *explicit* learning goals and activities led most to revise this view and question their own understanding of 'ideas about science' and the specific learning goals which could be set.

Teachers worked with us to produce activities and approaches to teach chosen 'ideas about science' explicitly and to further their own understanding of the area. We presented lesson outlines in which specific learning goals drawn from particular themes were embedded in activities selected from a range of existing sources (for example,

Lederman and Abd-El-Khalick 1998; Ratcliffe 1999). Teachers worked in age-specific groups to share and develop these, and their own ideas, in order to be able to implement specific lessons on the same 'idea about science' within teaching units on a range of science topics. Curriculum resources drawn upon included those aimed at development of ideas with similarity to the themes: *Charis Science* (Charis Project 2000); *AKSIS (ASE/King's Science Investigation in Schools) Project* materials (Goldsworthy *et al.* 2000); concept cartoons (Naylor and Keogh 2000); student texts and readers (for example, Heslop *et al.* 2000; Feasey 2001); and videos showing historical case studies of famous scientists and their work. In addition to completing questionnaires focusing on their understanding and preferred teaching style, teachers completed reflective diaries on their planning and delivery of lessons. We also kept field notes of discussions during the six days of meetings with teachers and conducted focus group discussions and individual interviews at the end of the project.

In working with us, teachers showed they could plan lessons and use teaching materials which addressed one or more themes through identification of learning goals and appropriate activities. For example, Emma, a primary teacher, indicated that in a particular lesson her intentions were to first discuss the nature of hypotheses and then 'I want them to go and make a hypothesis about the falling concept' (reflective diary entry). Jo, in teaching a lower secondary class, wrote these learning objectives on the board at the start of the lesson: 'By the end of this lesson you should know that: scientists often work collaboratively; scientists make hypotheses and predictions; scientists use experiments to test their ideas and that controls are important in those experiments' (observational field notes). In both cases these goals were set in the context of the science content of the topic being studied. Teachers thus chose learning activities which had the potential for student engagement with specific 'ideas about science'.

It was, however, immediately clear from classroom observation of teachers' attempts to teach lessons on the 'ideas about science' themes that the quality of students' engagement with specific 'ideas about science' was influenced less by the teaching materials and learning goals and more by the teachers' teaching styles and actions. Thus the focus of enquiry shifted from the evaluation of learning outcomes to exploring the factors influencing teachers' pedagogic effectiveness.

Detailed data analysis focused on the characteristics that distinguished effective from less effective lessons. Three overarching criteria were used in defining effective lessons – that essential components of such lessons should be: (a) a clear opportunity for students to consider explicitly elements of one theme or more; (b) student engagement with the topic at hand; and (c) student engagement in dialogue *about* science, i.e. the construction and evaluation of reasoned arguments that related ideas to the supporting evidence. Comparison of lessons which had these components with those in which one or more was absent allowed identification of features of teachers' actions which encouraged students' learning. The analysis led us to identify a series of 'dimensions' which can be used to characterise and describe the variation in lessons designed to teach an 'idea about science' (Figure 7.2). These dimensions are not mutually independent. They can, however, be used as an interpretative tool for locating and distinguishing teachers' practice, accepting that a given teacher may change position on a dimension as her/his teaching develops. Locating the eleven teachers on these dimensions suggests that for many teachers, used to traditional science teaching, effective explicit teaching of 'ideas about science' requires: a shift in the conception of their own role from dispenser of knowledge to facilitator of learning; a change in their classroom discourse to one which is more open and dialogic; a shift in their conception of the learning goals of science lessons to one which incorporates the develop-ment of reasoning as well as the acquisition of knowledge; and the development of activities that link content and process in tasks whose point and value is apparent to their students (Bartholomew *et al.* 2004).

It is useful at this point to consider the extent to which teachers' practice in addressing a particular 'idea about science' could be regarded as research evidence-informed. In presenting some lesson outlines and activities to teachers, we were drawing on research evidence. Some of the curriculum materials we shared were outcomes of research projects in which specific learning goals were identified and activities developed and evaluated to address these (Ratcliffe 1999; Goldsworthy *et al.* 2000). Similarly, we presented and discussed the use of some specific activities developed by researchers 'to help students make the crucial distinction between observation and inference, and appreciate the tentativeness of scientific knowledge and the role of creativity in science' (Lederman and Abd-El-Khalick 1998: 85). We were able to highlight to teachers specific learning goals which would be achieved through using such tasks. Thus, the teachers' practice had the potential to be research evidence-informed.

In teaching particular lessons, teachers did draw on the materials presented in these planning sessions. For example, Clare, a secondary teacher, taught a lesson with a focus on students making predictions

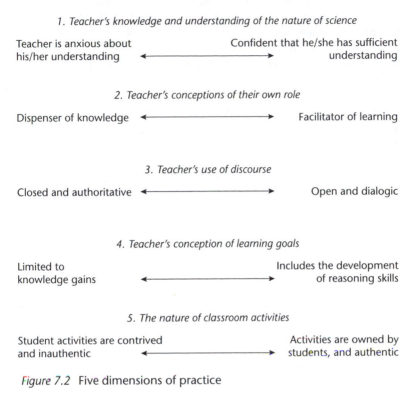

1. Teacher's knowledge and understanding of the nature of science

Teacher is anxious about
his/her understanding ⟷ Confident that he/she has sufficient
understanding

2. Teacher's conceptions of their own role

Dispenser of knowledge ⟷ Facilitator of learning

3. Teacher's use of discourse

Closed and authoritative ⟷ Open and dialogic

4. Teacher's conception of learning goals

Limited to
knowledge gains ⟷ Includes the development
of reasoning skills

5. The nature of classroom activities

Student activities are contrived
and inauthentic ⟷ Activities are owned by
students, and authentic

Figure 7.2 Five dimensions of practice

about what would happen to the mass of a sample of magnesium when heated in air, and testing to see if their predictions were correct and agreed with a theory they had been given (Goldsworthy *et al.* 2000). Clare focused extensively on the terminology of 'prediction', 'hypothesis' and 'theory' in introducing the lesson. Although the activity was informed by research evidence, the way in which Clare used the activity did not, however, allow students to engage fully with relevant 'ideas about science'. For example, in leading a question-and-answer session about the results of students' practical work, she asked for their opinions about their results but did not open up a more critical discussion of the extent to which their evidence supported or challenged their prediction. Her planning for the lesson (reflective diary) showed her concern that, in opening up an evaluative discussion, she might lose direction and control. In a normal class discussion, she would check the science content learnt. In considering specific 'ideas about science', she showed less clarity, asking: 'Just how are you supposed to sum that sort of thing [nature of science] up . . . not knowing what point it is you want to make in the sum up?' (interview). In this example, Clare's use of discourse and conception of learning goals tended to the left-hand side of these two dimensions (Figure 7.2).

Jo, also a secondary teacher, was able, on the other hand, to articulate specific learning goals to her students based on the themes. For example, a learning outcome written on the board at the start of a lesson was: 'Know that scientists use experiments to test ideas, but the result of a single experiment is rarely enough to prove an idea'. As in Clare's lessons, activities linked 'ideas about science' with the current scientific knowledge being taught – in this case an experiment on photosynthesis was used to examine the extent to which students could draw valid and reliable conclusions from their data. Jo was able to encourage more evaluative discussion among students than Clare, using small groups with focused questions and activities. This difference could not, however, be said to be a reflection of greater use by Jo of research evidence but rather of the variation amongst teachers in pedagogic style and approach, along the five dimensions of Figure 7.2.

As a further contrast, Andrew, a primary teacher, had great difficulty in focusing on specific learning goals in the activities he undertook and, consequently, in supporting students' learning. This was despite the exemplification of learning goals in sample lessons and his use of particular teaching materials. In an interview, he indicated, 'I would have liked to have tied my lessons in more tightly. . . . I think I needed to be more certain about how I could tie a specific theme into the sort of science topic we were doing.' These comments about his uncertainty contrast with his more sophisticated understanding of the nature of science than some other teachers' (questionnaire evidence). Thus, although Andrew had a good understanding of the nature of science, his position on the other dimensions of Figure 7.2 limited students' learning.

These examples are just a small sample from the data collected. There was little evidence overall, from observations of the lessons as they were enacted (the 'implemented' curriculum) or from teachers' reflections, that specific pieces of research evidence informed teachers' practice in addressing specific learning goals. In terms of the aspects of teachers' professional knowledge identified in Figure 1.1 in Chapter 1, our intervention appeared to be making teachers reflect on aspects of their professional knowledge base rather than on specific research findings.

Explicit teaching of 'ideas about science' encouraged teachers to question their understanding of the nature of science, their use of specific activities and their teaching strategies. The five dimensions of practice in Figure 7.2, emerging from the research, identify factors which need to be addressed in professional development designed to improve explicit teaching of 'ideas about science'. The main value of such research, therefore, lies more in providing a body of evidence to inform strategic decisions about the provision of continuing professional development for teachers than it does in informing the specific practices of these teachers.

Evaluation of students' learning – the 'attained' curriculum

Just as we can reflect on the extent to which specific teaching interventions were research evidence-informed, we can also consider the extent to which we drew upon research evidence in developing assessment tools to 'measure' students' learning of 'ideas about science'. Two approaches to measuring learning gains were tried: development of tests to address specific aspects of 'ideas about science', and students' completion of questionnaires to evaluate the nature and extent of their own learning from individual lessons. The latter proved problematic to collect. Teachers were provided with short questionnaires for students to complete at the end of each target lesson. There was not always the time, or the willingness on the part of teachers, to administer these questionnaires. The expected set of student evaluations was, thus, partial and not open to systematic analysis. The former approach, however, allowed data collection across all classes.

In order to get some measure of the learning gains of students within the target classes, teachers administered pre- and post-tests of understanding of some 'ideas about science' to students. The tests consisted of items with different response types (multiple choice; short answer; extended answer) which together addressed aspects of the nine themes from the Delphi study. These tests had been developed as part of a previous research project to explore the feasibility of using written test items for large-scale testing of students' understanding of 'ideas about science' (Osborne and Ratcliffe 2002). They were based on a systematic analysis of existing instruments to highlight their strengths and weaknesses in assessing specific learning goals. The instruments analysed had generally been used in research studies exploring students' understanding in the absence of focused teaching, and in many cases were used outside the classroom context. We refined existing items and developed new ones to try to assess specific learning goals, such as: ability to recognise or explain the terms 'hypothesis', 'theory' and 'experiment'; ability to use evidence to construct an argument about 'how we know'; and ability to evaluate data to identify patterns and conclusions. So these assessment items, like those developed in EPSE Project 1 (see Chapter 3), were research evidence-informed.

The pre-test and post-test had the same format. For example, one item in both tests was a comprehension passage in which students had to identify statements as hypotheses, observations or theories. Another item took the form of data analysis in which students had to evaluate evidence in formulating a conclusion. Although the skills being assessed were the same in both tests, the contexts were different. Besides being administered to each of the eleven target classes, the post-test was also given to a parallel class in each school. This allowed us to compare outcomes of each target class with a group at a similar educational stage and background but who had not experienced explicit teaching of 'ideas about science'.

An illustration of the kinds of issues involved in assessing 'ideas about science' is provided by discussion of the item shown in Figure 7.3, in which students are asked to evaluate experimental data. This item was adapted from research on ways of supporting students in undertaking their own investigations and analysing the resulting data (Goldsworthy *et al.* 2000). The item had face validity, as judged by independent science educators and teachers, for assessing graphical interpretation and pattern seeking. To evaluate the performance of all test items, the tests were administered to a large sample of 13-year-old students in twelve different schools (Osborne and Ratcliffe 2002). The facility value and discrimination index of different parts of this item are shown in Table 7.1. The facility value indicates the proportion of the population answering correctly. The discrimination index is a measure of how well performance on this item correlates with performance on the test as a whole. It is the difference between the proportion of students in the top 27 per cent on the test as a whole who get this item correct, and the proportion of students in the bottom 27 per cent on the test as a whole who do so. Reliable tests have high discrimination values. Ebel and Frisbie (1991) suggest that a discrimination index greater than 0.4 indicates a very good item, whilst one below 0.19 shows a poor item.

The first two parts of the item proved surprisingly demanding for all classes, with the second part showing poor discrimination. The later parts of the item were more accessible and discriminating. We

Read the information and answer the questions
Some pupils were investigating whether there was a pattern between people's
pulse rate and the number of breaths they take.
The scatter graph for their results is shown below.

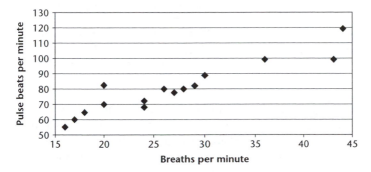

a) They tried to describe the pattern. Look at what they said below and
    complete each box with a YES or NO to answer the question at the top.

What the pupils said	Does it mention both factors?	Does it describe the general pattern?	Does it indicate that data from some individuals does not fit the pattern?
	YES or NO	YES or NO	YES or NO
(i) One pupil had the most breaths and she also had the highest pulse rate.	[YES]	[NO]	[NO]
(ii) All the people with a high breath rate had a high pulse rate.	[YES]	[NO]	[NO]
(iii) The higher your breathing rate, the greater the pulse rate.	[YES]	[YES]	[NO]
(iv) On the whole, those people with a higher breath rate had a higher pulse rate.	[YES]	[YES]	[YES]

b) Which one do you think was the best description? Explain your answer.
[Answer (iv), because it mentions both factors, describes the pattern and
indicates that it is not true for all cases. Others omit one or more of these.]

Figure 7.3 Item from post-test for secondary students (with expected
              answers in square brackets)

Table 7.1 Performance of item shown in Figure 7.3 in a large-scale trial with 13-year-old students (n=169)

	Part of item				
	a(i)	a(ii)	a(iii)	a(iv)	b
Facility value	0.32	0.14	0.51	0.46	0.34
Discrimination index	0.26	0.10	0.49	0.56	0.54

take these large-scale results to indicate that the item is reliable, with the exception of part a(ii). Other items in the tests also showed high reliability in the large-scale trial. It would be valuable, however, for there to be further development of appropriate assessment tools, along the lines of the research outlined in Chapter 3, as assessment of specific learning goals related to 'ideas about science' is in its infancy.

Inspection of responses to the same item in the post-test used for target and comparison classes shows that facility levels follow the pattern found in the large-scale trial (Table 7.2). There is, however, no obvious pattern of differences between target and comparison classes. Had the teaching of interpretation of data in the target classes been sustained and effective, we might have expected to see generally higher performance in these classes. On the tests overall, there was no statistically significant difference between the pre- and post-test scores in any of the target classes, nor between the post-test scores of target classes and the comparison classes. Although specific 'ideas about science' were addressed explicitly, for various reasons, including the infrequent teaching of some of the themes, this did not result in measurable learning gains. As we have illustrated above, teachers' preferred teaching styles and actions appeared to have considerable effect on the teaching of 'ideas about science'.

Although unable to pinpoint students' learning gains, we were left with a sense of less tangible benefits to students from their teachers' efforts. This was reinforced by teachers' comments on students' learning gains. Teachers described students' learning in relation to the 'ideas about science' themes using phrases like, 'they understand how scientists develop their ideas and have an awareness that scientists disagree about how to interpret the same evidence', and 'science is more closely linked to their real world and is constantly developing'. The change in students was seen as subtle and was demonstrated in the development of more

Table 7.2 Facility values of each part of the item shown in Figure 7.3 for students in target and comparison classes

	Part of item				
	a(i)	a(ii)	a(iii)	a(iv)	b
15-year-olds, school A Target	0.33	0.13	0.80	0.80	0.60
15-year-olds, school A Comparison	0.29	0.24	0.71	0.57	0.57
15-year-olds, school B Target	0.28	0.16	0.36	0.36	0.16
15-year-olds, school B Comparison	0.23	0.08	0.15	0.15	0.08
13-year-olds, school C Target	0.32	0.19	0.74	0.71	0.61
13-year-olds, school C Comparison	0.36	0.23	0.64	0.50	0.41
12-year-olds, school D Target	0.57	0.10	0.23	0.30	0.27
12-year-olds, school D Comparison	0.19	0.12	0.12	0.23	0.08
12-year-olds, school E Target	0.25	0.05	0.30	0.30	0.15
12-year-olds, school E Comparison	0.45	0.25	0.25	0.35	0.30
12-year-olds, school F Target	0.18	0.23	0.23	0.23	0.09
12-year-olds, school F Comparison	0.10	0.05	0.19	0.14	0.10

critical discussion by students. Teachers saw, as major benefits of teaching 'ideas about science' explicitly, an increase in students' interest brought about by using case studies of contemporary science which students saw as relevant and interesting.

Reflections: Developing research evidence-based practice

The detailed discussions in the previous sections have shown that we can claim that the 'intended' curriculum and the 'implemented' curriculum in this study are to some extent research-evidence informed. The Delphi study provided evidence that certain curricular goals command widespread agreement, but the development of specific learning targets to reflect these goals is a more taxing process. Negotiation with teachers as to what specific and feasible learning outcomes might follow from the initial broad themes led to a diverse set of outcomes and a correspondingly diverse set of lesson interventions. Without more precisely agreed learning outcomes and more specifically targeted interventions, it is difficult to produce appropriate instruments to evaluate the 'attained' curriculum. While it has been possible to outline learning goals and assessment measures for a few specific aspects of the 'ideas about science' themes, such as the interpretation of data, it has not proved feasible within the resources of this project to do this systematically across all the learning goals which might be seen as implicit in the 'ideas about science' themes. This study reinforces the view expressed in earlier chapters, that a key element in developing research-evidence based practice – determining clear learning outcomes and appropriate ways of measuring them – is a major undertaking. This is especially so in reflective domains such as 'ideas about science'.

Research evidence-based practice requires that we have a teaching intervention that can be implemented reasonably consistently by different teachers and in different classes. There are at least two major difficulties in designing such an intervention in the complex area of 'ideas about science'. One of these is choosing the science context within which a particular 'idea about science' will be developed. Our current study has not addressed the issue of choice of context, other than showing that several different subject knowledge contexts are feasible, and probably desirable, for any particular 'idea-about-science.' A more serious difficulty is limited understanding of what constitutes effective pedagogical content knowledge in relation to a specific learning outcome in the domain of 'ideas about science'. The provision of a teaching intervention in the form of curriculum materials to be implemented in a given way assumes that teachers recognise and have expertise in the particular pedagogy encouraged. It is apparent from our study that, if a teaching intervention were to be designed which emphasised pedagogy in line with the right-hand side of dimensions in Figure 7.2, many science teachers would be insufficiently familiar with the methods advocated to implement the intervention as intended.

We would argue that the outcome of our work with participating teachers is not yet an example of research-evidence based practice. That target is still a considerable way off. However, the study has shown clearly the pedagogical challenges and the ways in which we can start to characterise practice which fully engages students in considering 'ideas about science'. It has also shown some of the complexities of conducting research which might generate evidence that is generalisable to other contexts. The value of the study has been in providing evidence which allows teachers to reflect on their current practice and identify areas for professional development in any modification of their pedagogy, rather than providing them with an intervention that has been shown to 'work'.

Summary

The nine themes identified by the Delphi study discussed in Chapter 2 formed the starting point for the development, along with a group of teachers, of a set of lessons, each addressing one specific theme. This drew on insights from research, leading to short interventions that were, as far as was possible, research evidence-informed. There are, however, fewer specific research findings to guide this process than in other more familiar areas of the science curriculum. When the interventions were implemented, the success of the resulting lessons seemed to depend on five factors: the teacher's own knowledge and understanding of the nature of science, their conception of the teacher's role (as provider of knowledge or facilitator of learning), the kind of discourse they enabled to occur (closed and authoritative or open and dialogic), their conception of learning goals (as knowledge only, or also including development of reasoning skills), and the 'authenticity' and 'level of ownership' by the class of the learning activities. The need to choose a science context within which to teach any 'idea about science' means that lessons designed to teach the same 'idea' can be very different. The diversity of lessons implemented further exacerbated the already difficult challenge of measuring learning outcomes precisely. Both factors pose a considerable challenge to the development of research evidence-based practice in this area of the curriculum.

Chapter 8

From evidence to impact
Users' perceptions of research and
its influence on their practices

The previous chapters have viewed the research–practice interface
from the researchers' perspective. In this chapter we turn to the
perceptions of research in science education of potential users of
that research. Research evidence that a particular teaching practice
is successful in achieving its intended outcomes (Chapter 5), or that
carefully designed teaching materials can stimulate the kinds
of changes in practice that the designers intended (Chapter 6), or
that certain factors are associated with more successful teaching
(Chapter 7), is of little value unless it is noted by the practitioner
community and regarded as credible. Even then there may be
barriers to practitioners' use of research evidence in modifying
their teaching. In one of the four projects undertaken by the
Evidence-based Practice in Science Education Research Network, we
interviewed a sample of practitioners, and held a series of focus group
discussions, to explore the extent to which practitioners in science
education think their practice is influenced by research, and to assess
the value they place on research in making everyday choices and
decisions. One aim was to identify factors which facilitate and inhibit
the use of research evidence, as this may be important in thinking
about how best to communicate research to practitioners.

Background

As discussed in Chapter 1, teachers draw on a range of types of
knowledge in the course of their everyday practice (Figure 1.1).

*Authored by Mary Ratcliffe, Hannah Bartholomew, Vicky Hames, Andy Hind,
John Leach, Robin Millar and Jonathan Osborne*

Educational research may have a direct or indirect influence on teachers' decisions and choices. Professional knowledge, including that of research, does not come from a single source. Reading may contribute to a teacher's knowledge base. The practice of teaching is, however, strongly influenced by local craft knowledge which is socially constructed and communally shared; 'like other learners, teachers construct their knowledge through social interaction with peers, through applying ideas in practice, and through reflection and modification of ideas' (Marx *et al.* 1998: 670). Several studies of reflective practice have focused on professional interactions and reflection within the school context (Day 1999; Turner-Bissett 1999) but without giving explicit consideration to influences of research knowledge. Few empirical studies have explicitly explored research as an element in teachers' professional knowledge base. An exception is the study by Barnett and Hodson (2001) of six exemplary science teachers. This suggests that, whilst research knowledge is used by teachers, it influences practice less than professional or pedagogical content knowledge based on experience. Models of reflective practice attempt to capture the complexity of individual decision making. In our work, we did not set out to evaluate the influence of all the sources of professional knowledge included in such models but rather to focus on the extent to which research processes and evidence influence practitioners' actions. In seeking teachers' and other science education practitioners' views of educational research, we were asking them to reflect on their practice and to consider the extent to which research evidence forms part of their professional knowledge base and could be an agent of change in their practice. This approach assumes that practitioners have the ability to reflect on their own practice in the interviews and focus group discussions, even though the knowledge on which it is based may sometimes be largely tacit, or difficult to articulate.

Some studies have shown the positive disposition of some teachers, particularly those in senior management positions, towards the influence of research findings on their practice in general (for example, Galton 2000; DETYA 2001). The implication of such studies is that many teachers are open to using research evidence to modify their practice. Knowledge of research findings is a first step. However, it would appear that developing knowledge of research methods and findings does not feature strongly in science teachers' views about the professional development they require (Shkedi 1998; Costa *et al.* 2000). Of course, there are teachers who do have extensive knowledge and experience of research, often gained through completion of a higher degree in education, through action research or collaborative work with researchers. Do such teachers have better access to, and make better use of, research evidence? There is some evidence that this might be the case from surveys and interviews with teachers in action research consortia (Cordingley 1999; Elliott 2000; McNamara 2002). Thus, in our study, teachers with and without research experience were included, in order to explore any differences in their perceptions of the impact of research on their practice.

We deliberately focused on practice in the teaching of *science*, for the reasons outlined in Chapter 1. Teachers of science are engaged in teaching a body of content and skills. They do this in a variety of professional contexts – to diverse groups of students and within a range of school settings. Despite this diversity, a characteristic feature of their practice is the subject they are teaching, and into which they have been socialised. In contrast, previous studies of research influence have tended to ignore subject-specific elements and explored research influence on teachers in general (DETYA 2001; McNamara 2002).

Research design

In our study, we used a combination of interviews and focus groups to explore views in depth. Some studies have relied on data collection through questionnaires, thus limiting the extent to which reasoning and views can be probed (Galton 2000). Others have undertaken case studies of a few teachers in great depth (Barnett and Hodson 2001). Our approach takes a middle way, providing depth of analysis whilst canvassing views from a representative sample of reasonable size.

We interviewed sixty-two practitioners and conducted six focus groups – three of primary teachers and three of secondary teachers. The interview sample consisted of:

- twenty-one experienced science teachers with no formal experience of research: ten primary (identified as P1 in extracts cited below) and eleven secondary (S1);
- twenty experienced science teachers with experience of research: eight primary (P2) and twelve secondary (S2);
- twenty-one other science education practitioners (SEP): four curriculum policy makers (from government bodies like the Qualifications and Curriculum Authority (QCA) and the Office for Standards in Education (OfSTED)), four textbook authors, four leading participants in recent science curriculum development

projects, eight providers of initial and in-service training from the higher education, local education authority and independent sectors, and one chief examiner. (Several others in the sample also had examining experience in addition to their main role.)

The interview began by seeking perceptions of the influence of research on interviewees' practice. We deliberately chose not to define 'research' at the beginning of the interview, but used a card sort activity later in the interview to elicit participants' views on research. Each card showed an activity that might or might not be construed as research. All of these activities involved gathering and analysis of data but with different purposes and conducted by different kinds of people (professional researchers, inspectors, advisers, teachers). Interviewees were asked whether they would classify each activity as research or not, and why. Our interest lay not so much in their choices as in the reasons for these. Subsequent questions explored the role interviewees saw for research in improving practice, where they would look for ideas to improve aspects of their practice, and how they would evaluate changes in their practice.

The focus groups complemented the interviews by exploring which research findings, if any, were seen as convincing and likely to stimulate a change in practice. The discussion aimed to establish teachers' perceptions of the extent to which research can provide general guidelines for practice, and their views on what counts as 'evidence' in relation to choices and decisions they might make in their everyday practice. To focus the discussion, we wrote eight short vignettes of real examples of educational research, each about one page in length, with a range of research foci and methods. Each vignette included a summary of possible implications for a particular science education practice and contained a reference to the published source, usually a journal article or research report. Participants were sent these vignettes in advance. Questions in the focus group stimulated discussion on:

- whether participants were familiar with the research outlined in the vignettes
- the extent to which they found the research convincing or credible, and why
- the ways in which the research in the vignettes might be likely to influence their practice.

Practitioners' perceptions

Rather than attempting here to summarise the outcomes of this study, we will focus more selectively on some points that relate particularly to issues raised in other chapters. Fuller reports of this study of practitioners' views of research are available elsewhere (Ratcliffe *et al.* 2004, 2005). In this chapter we will look particularly at:

- teachers' perceptions of the influence of research on their teaching of science
- the characteristics of research evidence that teachers see as persuasive (and perhaps as requiring a change in practice)
- how teachers would evaluate a change in their own practice.

In the account that follows, all subjects' names are pseudonyms. The paragraph number after each quotation locates the passage in the transcript of each interview or focus group discussion.

Teachers' perceptions of the influence of research on their teaching of science

Teachers' views of the influence of research on their practice indicate the extent to which they feel it is already research evidence-informed or research evidence-based. Almost every interviewee said that they thought research did influence their practice, though views differed widely as to how large its influence was. A small number of teachers considered research to be a major influence:

> I'd put it as quite a major one really. . . . It is an area which I possibly want to go into myself, because I'm so fascinated by it. I love the idea of lifelong learning, always finding out more.
>
> (Colin, P1, para. 56)

Few were specific, however, about how their teaching was influenced by research, pointing to very general aspects. Ken (S2), for example, rated the influence of research as 'enormous. I'm a much better teacher now than I was. Much more tolerant' (para. 36). Some who felt that the influence of research was substantial also noted that its influence was often 'hidden' or invisible:

> I think, probably, research does have a big effect. But because I'm not using it directly, I'm not regarding it as a big effect, do you

know what I mean? I feel that I'm sort of down the line from it, you know.

(Janice, P1, para. 202)

A high proportion of the teachers who saw research as a major influence on their practice had had some personal experience of research. Most teachers with no personal experience of research saw it as a relatively minor influence on their practice. The following two responses are typical of others:

> I'd say, probably, a relatively modest influence.
>
> (Ursula, P1, para. 115)

> I: Do you think that what you do in your teaching is influenced by research?
> T: Not much. Very little I would say, these days.
>
> (Tony, S1, para. 16)

Again, some in this group saw research as playing an indirect or 'hidden role' (Louise, P1, para. 226). Sally (S1), for example, who saw the influence of research as 'relatively minor', commented:

> I'm unaware of things that I might use that I've found out from research. I may absorb things from staff or training days or courses that have been found out or are based on research, but I'm not really aware.
>
> (Sally, S1, para. 42)

Most interviewees and focus group participants therefore indicated or implied that research had some influence on their practice. It is difficult to gauge, from these initial responses alone, the extent to which the practice of such teachers could be said to be research evidence-informed. They appear open to considering research evidence and to view it as a positive influence. Further questions then explored in more detail their perceptions of the ways in which research might influence their practice. A small number of interviewees were able to give an example of a specific and direct influence of research on their teaching. If we can take teachers' expressed views as an accurate reflection of their practice, then some teachers do act on research evidence to modify their practice. Carol, for example, reported that:

One piece of research I'd read suggested, contrary to all I'd always thought, sit the boys together. So I thought OK, I'll give that a go and see what happens, and in the class that I had two years ago, a Year 2 class, I tried that for a while. I altered my seating arrangements to see what would happen.

(Carol, P2, para. 53)

Examples of a direct influence of research on practice were, however, mostly about general teaching or organisational strategies, such as ways of grouping pupils, rather than ways of teaching specific science topics, ideas or skills. Even those who cited particular pieces of research as influential were often unable to identify clearly the impact on their actions. For example, Richard referred to:

. . . research by Lovell that I was exposed to when I was training . . . about the intuitive control of variables, the fact that students perhaps up to the age of 16, the average student is unable to consciously control one variable. That pervades a lot of work that I do, course work, experimental planning and that kind of thing.

(Richard, S1, para. 20)

He was not, however, able to describe how his practice took these ideas into account. Even when teachers indicated they were aware of research in specific areas, their lack of comment on how this research had affected their teaching suggests that knowledge of research is just a first step; a significant and challenging task remains in adapting and using its findings or insights in a practical and effective manner in the classroom. Simply making teachers more aware of research, and better informed about it, is therefore unlikely to lead to significant or widespread changes in practice.

A more widespread perception, coming out of both interviews and focus groups, is that research influences teaching by less direct means. Major research projects which had produced output in the form of curriculum resources and teaching materials were commonly mentioned as ways in which research informs and influences everyday practice. In over half of all interviews and focus group discussions, one or more research-based projects such as *CASE (Cognitive Acceleration through Science Education)*, *AKSIS (ASE/King's Science Investigations in Schools)* and *CLISP (Children's Learning in Science Project)* were spontaneously mentioned. Teachers recognised these as outputs of research projects. But their comments suggest that it was the materials rather than the research evidence that they valued. Adoption of the materials tends to precede any consideration of the research evidence. For example, Patrick talked of the extent of change involved in taking on a research-informed teaching intervention, but did not mention the research evidence about its outcomes as a factor in deciding to make this change:

> Originally, CASE . . . came to us just as . . . thirty lessons . . . They were a very different style to the way that most of us were used to teaching. But gradually we learned, and from going and finding out about the research, we learned that it had the biggest knock-on effect if it affected your whole teaching strategy.
>
> (Patrick, S1, para. 21)

Hazel expressed very clearly a view shared by several others that new teaching interventions are adopted primarily because of their perceived usefulness, with research evidence playing at best a supporting role:

> When we talk about it we wouldn't think to ourselves 'oh, my word, we are using research now'. We think this is a good idea and it fits in with our ethos and so we will try it. We will do that first and then we might look at the research findings that have backed it up. But we wouldn't look at research first and say 'oh, there are so many more improved results, therefore we will do it'.
>
> (Hazel, S2, para. 54)

The subordinate role of research also emerged when practitioners were asked where they would seek advice and ideas for improving an aspect of their practice. No interviewee spontaneously identified research as the source to which they would first look. Most referred instead to:

> . . . talking to colleagues, that's a vital interchange of ideas, I think, in terms of I tried this and it worked really well, or I tried that and it fell flat on its face, or whatever.
>
> (Pauline, S1, para. 28)

Often colleagues, local authority advisers, or other in-service providers were seen as having knowledge or experience of research, and many interviewees saw this as an important means by which research influenced practice. Theresa, for example, talked of sharing information with colleagues about a piece of research which had impressed her:

> I went on a course, some years ago now and it's the first time that
> I came across 'Inside the Black Box' about formative assessment and
> the research on that, and I was particularly interested in that
> and so I circulated the information.
>
> (Theresa, S2, para. 35)

These examples suggest that one important means of transforming
practice is by offering resources, instruments and strategies which
teachers, as a community, value and may adopt – accepting that even
where these are informed by research, users may be unaware of this
influence. Some research in social psychology suggests that changing
behaviours depends on first changing beliefs and attitudes (Ajzen and
Fishbein 1980). Others, however, have shown how changes in practice,
even those imposed from outside, can lead to changes in opinions and
values, if they are judged with hindsight to have had beneficial effects
(Vulliamy 2004; Webb et al. 2004). Thus research-informed teaching
materials, if designed in such a way that teachers can quickly see their
potential usefulness, may be a particularly effective bridge between
research and practice.

Teachers' judgement of research evidence as persuasive of a change in practice

Teachers' views on educational research provide an insight into their
understanding of educational research methods and of the kind of
knowledge it can produce. These views may help to identify some of the
obstacles to the direct use of research evidence. At a general level, in
distinguishing between activities they had classified as research and
non-research, interviewees argued that research was: enquiry with a
purpose in mind; carried out in a systematic and objective manner (often
using controls or comparisons); intended to inform action; and more
credible if it was large scale. In contrast, activities classified as 'not
research' were characterised as: just collecting information; part of
normal practice; subjective; or small scale. Commonly, as in the two
extracts below, interviewees used just one or two of these features to
justify their classification of each activity discussed:

> It's for a purpose . . . you're trying to establish some good practice
> or other. You're trying to improve your teaching or . . . your
> resources.
>
> (Nancy, S2, para. 156)

Research involves more than just one group, it should have different groups of . . . children or whatever . . . to have perhaps a control group and compare how those groups would do in different circumstances, and what would impact on that, and then hopefully draw a conclusion to answer the hypothesis.

(Ursula, P1, para. 87)

Many teachers without research experience professed limited under-standing of criteria for evaluating research studies or their findings, notwithstanding their willingness to comment generally on purpose and methods. Some features of research were notable by their absence. For example, no interviewee suggested that a research enquiry should have a clear theoretical or conceptual framework, although five (like Ursula above) did argue that having a prior hypothesis was an important criterion. The dominant emphasis was on systematic empirical enquiry – comparing cases, or seeking evidence of correlations that might indicate possible causal links. For some this was seen as making the research 'scientific'. As Louise put it:

. . . the idea of control classes. For me tends to put it more on a scientific sort of basis.

(Louise, P1, para. 148)

On most issues, differences between teachers with and without research experience were not great. Those with research experience did, however, tend to articulate clearer views on the nature of research and were somewhat more prepared to envisage research taking a variety of forms, from individual action-research to large-scale studies. A teacher with research experience was clearly taking a broader view of research in putting all the card sort activities into the 'research' category:

I would say that all of them [the activities on the cards], in a sense, could come under research, small scale, and I know some teachers or LEA advisers doing their Master's or whatever would be expected to do some very small-scale [research]. . . . I think these are . . . generating new knowledge, from the data and from practice.

(Ralph, P2, para. 42)

From the interviews as a whole, there appears to be no single common, or even dominant, view of the criteria that make an enquiry 'research' in science education. Rather, different activities are seen as research by different interviewees, provided they fulfil the central criteria of having a clear purpose and a systematic approach. About a third of interviewees mentioned both of these, and most of the remainder mentioned one. Many responses from all groups lacked specific detail, suggesting for instance that data should be collected systematically but saying little about issues such as validity and reliability.

The views of educational research held by teachers of science suggest that many are quite strongly influenced by their experiences or knowledge of research *in science*. Many, indeed, seem to have a rather idealised view of this, and show little awareness that medical research, for instance, 'typically uses small sample experimental research as the basis for establishing the possibilities of effects' and that 'researchers recognise that mixed methods of research serve complementary purposes' (Darling-Hammond and Youngs 2002: 15). Those who had themselves engaged in educational research were more prepared to accept as appropriate, and to see as 'research', a range of methods and designs. Many teachers appeared to lack a clear understanding of social science research, of its differences from research in the natural sciences, and of appropriate criteria for making judgements about its claims. Rather, their ideas were based either on models of empirical enquiry and hypothesis testing borrowed from the physical sciences, or on more diffuse lay conceptions of enquiry.

The rigour of research methods and the scale and scope of data collection were also features which focus group teachers commented on in judging whether the research outcomes presented in vignettes could be regarded as convincing. For example, small-scale studies were dismissed as providing insufficient evidence:

> T: A class of five, it's not enough.
> I: So what would convince you?
> T: Well you'd want to see something similar done in a variety of different schools with, you know, normal schools . . .
> > (secondary focus group 1, para. 139–141)

> It's not a convincing piece of research when you have such a small sample. Especially a hand-picked sample, presumably. And not necessarily with your ordinary, average teacher either . . .
> > (secondary focus group 1, para. 386)

Focus group discussions also explored the extent to which findings might persuade teachers of the need to make a change in their practice.

In all focus groups, some teachers said they would want to know contextual and background information before making a judgement about a piece of research, particularly if the claims made by the research appeared vague, or 'too good to be true'. The following comment on one vignette is an example of this view:

> I just thought when I first read this . . . that there were just so many questions that I wanted to ask about it. So I've put it also as 'some reservations'. I wanted to know more about the groups who did it and whether you have to do all thirty of them to get those – lots of those sorts of questions. I'm quite prepared to believe the trials, I just need a bit more back-up information.
>
> (secondary focus group 1, para. 79)

In making judgements about the extent to which findings can be generalised and, in particular, applied to their own context, several focus group members referred to the complexity of human behaviour:

> T: I mean children are so complex, the human personality's so complex that it's so difficult, isn't it? I mean, the government can't decide on MMR, which is reasonably straightforward compared with most educational research, it's hardly surprising we can't agree that something done in a classroom a hundred miles away is going to apply to our classroom.
> T: Yeah, but there's medical research, very sort of definite evidence, isn't there? Not that there isn't in educational research, but the nature of the evidence is a lot different, a lot more open to interpretation.
>
> (primary focus group 3, para. 600–602)

The important issue here may be the clarity of the outcome measure. In many medical situations, the outcome is clear-cut; the medical condition of the patient either improves or does not. In educational situations, the judgement as to whether better learning occurred, and the measurements that support this, are significantly more complex.

Although issues of generalisability and methodological considerations (such as the use of comparisons and controls) were prominent in the discussion of what counts as research and as 'good research', one other factor was mentioned very frequently in discussing how persuasive a specific research finding was. Many teachers referred to the extent to which a finding resonated with their own experience, or was in line with their views and beliefs, or with their department's policy and practice:

> I tend to look at things that I can often relate to as either currently in my practice, or [. . .] that's happened to me, and that's a good way of solving that.
>
> (primary focus group 1, para. 244)

> I'm not convinced of the one about the less able pupils [vignette 3]. . . . I'm less convinced about that because of my experiences being the opposite.
>
> (primary focus group 3, para. 396)

Thus, as Kennedy (1997) has also noted, research seems more likely to influence practice when the findings accord with experience or beliefs. The tendency for research findings to be used as confirmation of existing practice was echoed in focus group discussion. Although many agreed that research findings could provide new knowledge, there was also a feeling that this was more likely to be accepted when it confirmed the value of existing practice. Such comments are in line with a large Australian study (DETYA 2001) which found that 'generally teachers seek out the sources they believe will build on their existing knowledge' (p. 2).

The implicit risk here is that research may convince practitioners only of things they believe they already know – with any surprising or unexpected findings being dismissed as 'unconvincing'. Teacher education may have an important role in helping teachers to reflect more deeply on the nature of enquiry in education, so as to arrive at a more considered view of what is possible, and what might count as 'sound evidence' on which to base actions and decisions.

How teachers evaluate a change in their practice

The strongly experimental view of educational research which many science teachers seem to hold might suggest that they would take a similar approach to evaluating changes in their own practice. The ways in which teachers say they would evaluate their own practice may also indicate their receptiveness to the idea that research findings might inform their practice, or that research could provide evidence to support specific choices and decisions about practice. More than three-quarters of the teachers interviewed talked about assessment of pupil attainment, in national tests and public examinations, as the most important evidence they would consider when evaluating a change in practice:

> . . . well, results obviously. Teacher assessments. So . . . at the end of a topic, say, some sort of formal assessment, national tests.
>
> (Yvonne, P1, para. 203)

> In terms of results it's fairly easy to gauge. We do keep all our records on a central computer from year to year so we can see if there is an improvement there.
>
> (Quentin, S2, para. 134)

The outcome indicators to which teachers referred were almost always *overall* measures of attainment in science, rather than measures directly related to a specific change. In addition to external tests, many also referred to less objective indicators of improved learning that might precede a summative assessment:

> It's usually a personal, subjective judgement, when you're actually teaching the subject that you feel they've got a far better understanding of it, and, when they do their assessment, the results which they produce there.
>
> (Jack, P1, para. 178)

Teachers referred to a range of indicators of improvement. Several identified students' reactions and responses during the teaching as their main indicator of success. In particular, the quality of verbal responses was highlighted:

> Personally it's generally from verbal feedback from kids. I'll question them and if they've picked up on what I've done or what they've done, and if I can see a change in the way that they are answering questions or the way they are talking back, then I'll think it's had an effect.
>
> (Ben, S2, para. 256)

> Well . . . you've got the gut feeling and the actions of the kids and the vocabulary they use, the kind of non-written signs and the more elaborate explanations they give, the kind of chronological or

sequencing or cognitive good thought processes you can see going on, there's that. The rounded feel you get to the lesson.

(Colin, P1, para. 227)

Richard referred in similar terms to quality of written work and evidence of ideas learned, but then went on to talk about pupil engagement and motivation; for many teachers, these were important indicators of improvement:

> Quality of work, written work, ideas. So if you felt there was an improvement to something in a lesson, you would hope that that was reflected in the work of the students in some way, perhaps in some written work, their ideas, the quality of work, the number of books that got handed in when you next wanted them in, that kind of thing. So there'd be all those kind of factors. . . . If there was an improvement then you would expect, with the attendance, that would be measurable. You'd expect punctuality. There'd be enthusiasm, there'd be less level of disruption, you know, all of those factors.
>
> (Richard, S1, para. 159)

For many practitioners this 'gut instinct' (Patrick S1, para. 124) came with experience and influenced how they prioritised, or even interpreted, different kinds of evidence in the decision-making process. The bases of professional judgement were difficult to articulate, but involved evaluation of pupils' reactions in various ways:

> It's difficult to describe it really. Sometimes you really know that it's really gone well . . . the feedback you get back from the students . . . And sometimes you really try to do something and it just falls flat and you think, why didn't that get a response? So you learn, I'm saying, I suppose, you learn through experience, through taking a risk, trying something new, seeing how it goes and taking it from there.
>
> (Pauline, S1, para. 164)

The picture that emerged from interviewees' comments on evaluation of change in their own practice is of professional judgement about the response of pupils to new methods and approaches, set against the background of an education system in which data on pupil attainment currently play a major role. Very few examples were given of systematic collection of specific evidence by teachers to reach conclusions about the effectiveness of a teaching intervention or innovation that they had chosen, or might choose, to adopt.

Channels of influence

From this study, we would highlight two main points about the interface between research and practice. One is about the ways in which research findings and insights may influence decisions and choices – resulting in these being different from what they would otherwise have been. The other is about the role of research evidence in making judgements about specific practices. The first is therefore about research evidence-informed practice, the second about research evidence-based practice, as we have used these terms (see Chapter 1, Figures 1.1 and 1.2).

Ways in which research might be said to influence practice can be divided into three categories:

- Specific (where knowledge of a specific research finding influences a particular piece of teaching)
- General (where research is believed to support the use of a certain teaching style or approach)
- Indirect (through using teaching materials, or following guidelines, that are considered to be informed by research).

The practitioners we interviewed gave very few examples of the first of these. Many made reference to the third. Whilst we might question the extent and depth of the 'research influence' on some of the teaching materials that are widely used, or the documents that set the framework for curriculum, assessment and teaching, examples of teaching materials that are clearly and explicitly informed by research were quite frequently mentioned. This suggests that the use of such materials may be one of the main ways in which research influences practice. Taken as a whole, our interview data suggest that research findings are much more likely to have an impact on practice if they are used (perhaps by researchers and practitioners working together) to develop teaching materials or guidelines that can be directly used in the classroom. Communication of findings may raise awareness and knowledge, but is less likely to result in actual changes in actions and choices.

In another sense, though, communication is vitally important. Many of those we interviewed talked of professional contacts, with colleagues, local authority advisers, teacher educators and researchers, as important in raising their awareness of research findings and approaches, helping them to identify developments that might be more worth attending to, and supporting them in trying out new approaches. Professional organisations, in particular the Association for Science Education, were often mentioned as important in this regard – and appear to play a key role in establishing and supporting a community of practice which values research, and seeks to use it as a resource to improve practice.

As regards the role of research in evaluating practices, there was a striking contrast between the rigour of the criteria that many teachers appeared to apply in evaluating given accounts of research, and those that teachers said they would apply in judging the success of changes in their own practice. Whilst general measures of attainment in science were mentioned by several teachers, many also appeared to base judgements on rather intuitive outcome 'measures' rather than on specific data. Professional judgement, based on experience, the 'feel' of a change, and the students' response, forms an important qualitative yardstick for teachers. It would appear that the yardstick many respondents use to judge the outcomes of research is significantly more demanding than that which they use to assess their own practice.

Finally, our findings suggest that any impetus towards research evidence-informed, or research evidence-based, practice is not coming from teachers. In one sense, this is unsurprising. Teaching involves a community of practitioners (Wenger 1998), and much of their knowledge of what constitutes good practice is embedded in social practices. However, the limited knowledge of research, and the relative weakness of the relationship between individuals' practice and research, suggest that the teaching of science is a somewhat closed practice – that is, one in which its practitioners do not expect their more detailed choices and decisions to be warranted by rigorous and systematically collected evidence. Other professions, like medicine, are much more reliant on research evidence to improve practice. A shift in perception, towards seeing teaching interventions as 'packages' designed to achieve specific goals, whose attainment can be measured, may be necessary for research to become a stronger influence on the day-to-day events of practice.

Summary

Many science teachers consider that research does influence their everyday actions, but see this influence in very general terms, or through the fact that they use structures (such as a national curriculum and 'official' schemes of work) or resources (such as textbooks), which they believe to be 'informed by research'. Communication of research findings to teachers has a limited impact on practice. Teachers, however, appear willing to modify their practice, and to use teaching strategies and materials based on research, when they can see the benefits of these in their own situation and believe they address current issues or concerns. Research evidence-informed practice is thus possible through targeted curriculum materials and approaches. Teachers' professional networks also seem important in involving teachers in a community of practice where research is valued. To encourage research evidence-based practice, there may need to be a stronger focus in initial and in-service teacher education on teachers' understanding of the strengths and limitations of educational research, so that more are able and confident to use evidence that has been systematically generated to evaluate their own and others' practice.

Part III

What are the overall implications?

Chapter 9

Improving practice in subject teaching

The contribution of research

We began this book with a series of questions: What contribution can research make to improving the teaching and learning of a school curriculum subject? Can research help us to improve the way subjects are taught, and the learning that ensues? If so, what kind of help can we reasonably expect research to provide: new information, perspectives or insights that we may need to consider and take into account, or clear and compelling evidence that certain interventions 'work' or do not? And exactly how should research be designed and carried out to provide the kind of knowledge that can lead to practical improvements? In this final chapter, we want to return to these broad questions about the contribution that research makes, or could make, to the improvement of practice in the teaching of a school curriculum subject such as science.

Teaching a curriculum subject

The Evidence-based Practice in Science Education (EPSE) Research Network chose to focus on the teaching and learning of a specific curriculum subject because this is the context of much of the everyday work of most teachers, whether they teach one subject at secondary level or several at primary level. Many of the day-to-day choices and decisions that a teacher makes are about how best to teach the topics and ideas their classes are currently working on. Some of these may not even be seen as choices but simply as the 'normal' way of doing things;

Authored by Robin Millar, John Leach, Jonathan Osborne and Mary Ratcliffe

others arise from conscious reflection. Either way, choices *are* always involved; any piece of teaching can be planned and staged in many different ways. If research is to have a significant impact on teachers' practices, then it must be able to influence decisions and choices *about the detail of teaching and learning*. The examples discussed in this book concern the teaching and learning of science. But the underlying issues about the role of research in informing educational practice are general. We see science as 'standing for' any subject of the school curriculum – providing a context within which general issues concerning the influence of educational research on practice are played out.

Improving practice, improving practices

The word 'practice' has a wide range of meanings. It can be used to refer very generally to the professional work of an individual or group, as when we talk of 'improving practice in science education'. A teacher's practice is, however, the sum of a large number of more specific 'practices': the procedures or approaches which he or she follows in carrying out specific tasks. These practices embody choices and decisions about curriculum and assessment (which shape and constrain what teachers are required to do) and about pedagogy (the ways in which they do them). We improve practice by improving specific practices.

'Practices' vary widely in type – from the general organisational choices and decisions that a school or department might make, to the much more particular choices and decisions that a teacher takes in planning and carrying out a specific piece of teaching, or which are embodied in the materials they use. Table 9.1 suggests one way of classifying types of educational 'practice'. The focus of much the EPSE Network's activity has been on content-specific practices of types D and E. These are not, however, clearly distinct from more 'generic' practices of types B and C. The latter often provide a major part of the design rationale for content-specific practices of types D and E. Conversely, generic practices of types B and C have to be implemented in the context of teaching *some* specific content (knowledge or skill). Any practical intervention based on them involves more detailed choices and decisions that depend on knowledge of, and views about, the chosen content. From the perspective of evaluation – of asking 'does it work?' – there is little practical difference between generic (types B and C) and content-specific (types D and E) practices. All we can ever evaluate is *a specific teaching intervention*. If one based on a generic approach is found to be effective, this may suggest that it would be worth extending the

Table 9.1 Types of educational 'practice'

	Type of 'practice'	Example
A.	A general aspect of organisation	Set maximum class size of 20 for certain subjects or pupil groups.
B.	A teaching approach that is applicable across subjects	Use formative assessment methods.
C.	A teaching approach that is generally applicable within a subject	Base science teaching on small-group practical work.
D.	An intervention for teaching a domain within a subject, to achieve specified learning objectives	Use a particular teaching scheme for a unit on plant nutrition.
E.	An intervention for teaching a key idea within a subject domain, to achieve a specified learning objective	Use a particular sequence of activities to teach the idea that electric current is the same everywhere around a series circuit.

approach to other topics and contents – but these would then need to be separately evaluated, as they will require different choices and decisions that relate to the new content.

There is one other type of practice (and intervention) which is not included in Table 9.1 – those practices designed to improve skills that are useful across subjects and topics. Examples might include 'thinking skills' or 'learning how to learn'. The *Cognitive Acceleration through Science Education (CASE)* project (Adey *et al.* 1996) is an example of a specific teaching intervention of this sort. For these it may be possible to show an impact on students' performance not only in the outcome measures specifically designed to evaluate the intervention but also in the much broader-brush measures used to assess student performance in subject areas. Indeed the high level of uptake of CASE in English schools can be substantially attributed to the evidence of its impact on students' scores in national tests and examinations across a range of subjects, rather than evidence of improvement on outcome measures (such as post-test and delayed post-test data) focusing on the more specific objectives of the intervention (Adey and Shayer 1990, 1993).

There are, however, relatively few interventions of this sort which are plausible candidates for improving learning 'across the board'. Improvement in the teaching and learning of a subject like science is perhaps as likely to come through improving the way in which specific topics, concepts, ideas and skills are taught. Our own observation of practice over many years leads us to believe that learning outcomes in many areas of science – and indeed the student experience of science learning – could be significantly improved through changes in the ways in which specific topics are commonly taught.

The question at the heart of the EPSE projects (and hence of this book) might therefore be stated as: 'How can research contribute to improving the teaching of X?' – where X is a particular topic, or idea, or concept, or skill. In attempting to answer it, we will use the distinction drawn in Chapter 1 and used in Chapters 2–8, between the influence of knowledge and ideas from research on the *design* of teaching interventions, and the extent to which research provides (or can provide) evidence about the *outcomes* of an intervention that would justify recommending teachers to adopt it. Teaching interventions whose design can be seen to have been influenced by research we term 'research evidence-informed'. Those for which there is research evidence about outcomes we term 'research evidence-based'. We will first explore the extent to which a current practice in science education might reasonably be termed 'research evidence-informed', and what might be involved in seeking to make it more so. We will then go on to consider the same questions about research evidence-based practice. Although we explore these issues in the context of teaching science, they apply more widely to the teaching of many school curriculum subjects.

First, however, one very general issue needs to be raised. This is the matter of what we might call 'grain size' – the size of the 'units' of teaching and learning that we are considering. If we are interested in improving the teaching and learning of X, and in the role that research might play in this, then what size should X be? An answer to this is implicit in the scope and scale of the projects we undertook, but it may be important now to make the reasons for these choices more explicit. Ultimately, of course, our aim as science educators is to improve the teaching and learning of science, but this is a very large target. If a new approach to school science were proposed, its evaluation would take years to complete. Any major new curriculum development is also likely to involve a change of emphasis – a somewhat different set of aims and goals – making a direct comparison of the old and new impossible. Also, any large intervention (needing more than, say, 10 lessons) is likely to draw on several theoretical ideas, or to have several design criteria, and will then involve many further decisions about how to implement these in the context of the chosen content. So even were we able to show that it 'worked' better than other approaches, we would not be sure which of its features were crucial to its success – and so could not easily apply this knowledge to design new teaching approaches for other contexts or situations.

If we want research to play a significant role in improving teaching and learning, and to generate the kind of knowledge on which improvement can be cumulatively built, we need to consider smaller 'units'. For these it is easier to identify the intended learning outcomes, as there are fewer of them, and to devise ways of assessing how far they are attained. A short teaching intervention is also likely to be based on a smaller number of design criteria, or theoretical ideas. So we are more likely to be able to get evidence of the value of these. From a practical perspective, the evaluation of a short intervention can be carried out more quickly, has less impact on normal routines, and carries lower risk for the students, teachers and schools involved. Thinking in terms of smaller, more tightly focused teaching 'units' is also the perspective on teaching and learning that the analogy with evidence-based medicine invites us to adopt. For a doctor deciding how to treat a patient, the relevant evidence is about the outcomes of different treatments of a *specific* illness or condition, not generic knowledge that would apply to the treatment of any illness. The educational equivalent is 'treating' a *specific* knowledge or skills deficit – a lack of understanding of a specific topic or idea, or an inability to carry out a specific procedure – and the outcomes of different interventions that might be used to remediate it. We are not arguing that all educational problems can be reduced to the evaluation of small, contained interventions with clear and specific aims. Rather we are suggesting that it is to questions and issues on this scale that research can most effectively contribute.

If we want to improve the teaching and learning of a subject by improving the way in which specific topics are taught and learned, it would clearly be sensible to focus on the topics and ideas that are of central importance to the subject, and which are recognised to pose the greatest difficulties for learners. In many science topics there are 'critical steps' which a learner has to surmount to make progress in understanding – and which, if not taken, are an obstacle to progress. These are, however, often insufficiently highlighted in curriculum specifications and teaching resources – and insufficiently differentiated from material that is less crucial for the development of understanding and which poses less significant learning demands for students. Johnson (2000), for example, has pointed out that the idea of a 'chemical substance', which is fundamental to the development of understanding in chemistry, is not mentioned in the English national curriculum (DfEE/QCA 1999) or in the semi-official teaching scheme (QCA 2000) that supports it – and hence is not emphasised in published textbooks and teaching resources. The fact that several of the teachers involved in EPSE Project 2 (Chapters 4–5) were unable to identify exactly where the ideas of 'chemical substance' and 'chemical reaction' were introduced in their school's teaching scheme corroborates this. And this is not an isolated example. Teaching schemes and textbooks do little to highlight ideas or concepts that merit or require particular attention and effort – either by giving them more time and space than other less important points, or flagging their importance in other ways. A prerequisite for evidence-based education is that we come to a clearer, and more generally agreed, view of the critical ideas or learning steps that are of greatest importance for the development of understanding in each subject – in order to be able to direct effort towards finding more effective ways of dealing with these.

The strategy of trying to improve the teaching and learning of a subject by improving the way in which specific key ideas or topics are taught and learned has some implications. One is that only in the longer term could we expect to see a measurable improvement in students' scores on the broad-brush instruments normally used to evaluate performance in curriculum subjects. These test knowledge and understanding across a whole subject, sampling it quite lightly, with the result that an improvement in the teaching and learning of any one topic is unlikely to make a marked difference to students' overall scores. This contrasts with interventions designed to develop skills that are applicable across many content domains (such as 'thinking skills'), which are expected to improve performance across topics and contents – and so may have a measurable effect on broader measures of performance. This has implications for the dissemination and uptake of short content-specific interventions. It may be harder to persuade practitioners that the effort of adopting a short content-specific intervention is worthwhile, even if it has been shown to lead to better scores on a measure of understanding of the topic or idea that it deals with.

Seeing overall improvement in the teaching of a subject in terms of improving the teaching of specific key topics and ideas within it might also be seen as implying a strongly goal-directed view of teaching. Donnelly (1999a) argues that teaching involves a tension between instrumentality (actions in pursuit of clearly recognised goals) and what he terms 'a concernful being-with children' (p. 933), in which goals are less well-defined or recognised. 'Being a teacher' does not then so much involve solving specific problems (such as correcting students' lack of knowledge or skill in a particular domain) as participating in a meaningful social practice in ways which become, with growing experience, increasingly taken-for-granted and unproblematic. This analysis highlights an important difference between teaching and the 'problem-solving' professions (such as medicine, nursing, law), where clients present with a 'problem' of some kind – the solution of which signals an endpoint of the professional encounter. In educational contexts, on the other hand, there is no single, agreed, final endpoint; any endpoint is provisional and may be the starting point for further learning. On the other hand, the very fact of compulsory education implies certain aims or intentions on society's part – and the curriculum and its assessment do define (often quite tightly) expectations of learners at a given age and stage. Learning science involves an induction into a specific way of looking at the world, learning how to view events and processes in terms of a framework of concepts and models that are consensually agreed within the scientific community, and how to construct appropriate arguments linking data and explanations. The corpus of knowledge is hierarchical, with more powerful ideas building upon more fundamental ones, implying an order in which learning can best take place. Science education can, perhaps to a greater extent than some other curriculum subjects, reasonably be seen as a largely goal-directed activity.

The contribution of research to the design of teaching interventions

Asking 'how can research contribute to improving the teaching of X?' implies, first, that we consider X to be worth teaching and learning. Can research say anything about this? Surely values, rather than evidence, underpin people's views on curriculum content. The first phase of EPSE Project 3 (see Chapter 2), however, shows how research can play a valuable role in the design and specification of a curriculum, by establishing the level of agreement about some of the choices involved. A Delphi study, involving individuals drawn from different groups that might be considered to have 'an interest' in curriculum choices, can identify themes or topics or ideas which are widely seen to merit inclusion. It can also tell us if key 'interest groups' have significantly different perspectives, leading to different views on curriculum content, or if variations of view *within* each group are as large as those *between* groups. Our Delphi study focused on an aspect of the science curriculum – teaching students about the nature of scientific knowledge and enquiry – where there is no established tradition and the 'curriculum definition' of the topic is still fluid. Similar issues arise, though they are often less apparent, with more established aspects of curriculum content. Here, too, the curriculum is always a choice from a much larger body of possible, and worthwhile, content. Recognising this, some reports on curriculum issues have argued that the decisions taken in prescribing content should be made more explicit, and that more be said to explain how they are considered to follow from the general aims of the curriculum (Millar and Osborne 1998). This is particularly necessary when more radical changes in curriculum rationale are envisaged. For example, the idea of 'scientific literacy' has become increasingly widely used, since the early 1990s, to argue that the school science curriculum should give greater emphasis to ideas and understandings that the ordinary citizen might find useful in everyday situations, and less to ideas that are really only required as a basis for later, more specialised courses in science, leading towards professional qualifications (Millar 1996; Bybee 1997; Goodrum *et al.* 2001). Whilst this viewpoint is based on values rather than empirical evidence, working out its more detailed implications requires such evidence. If our aim is to equip students better to deal with scientific information in the forms in which they encounter it outside the classroom, then curriculum planning could benefit greatly from a detailed and thorough analysis of the contexts and situations in which scientific ideas are encountered, of the forms in which scientific information is presented, and of the knowledge and skills needed to deal appropriately with it. Only a few empirical studies of this sort exist (Ryder 2001; Tytler *et al.* 2001). Were more available, the specification of curriculum content could become much more research evidence-informed. Research therefore offers a way of making the processes of curriculum specification and design more transparent. Whilst such research would tell us little about learning outcomes, it might significantly clarify the outcomes which might in time be evaluated through research of a different kind.

Asking 'how can research contribute to improving the teaching of X?' also implies that aspects of how X is currently taught are unsatisfactory. For many Xs that are generally considered central to the science curriculum, there is much research evidence that this is so. A large, international programme of research (see Duit 2006) has documented in detail the ideas and misconceptions that students typically hold about different aspects of the natural world, and the difficulty of changing many of these to bring them more closely into line with the accepted scientific view. So, for example, there are many research studies of students' ideas about matter, light, electricity, how and why things move, physiological processes in plants and animals, and so on. Likewise there are many studies on learning how to read, and on the difficulties that children have with specific aspects of mathematics. The importance and value of this research as a resource for improving practice is considerable. Recognising a problem, and defining it more precisely, are essential precursors to remediating it. The research programme on learners' conceptions of the natural world has taken what would otherwise be local and anecdotal knowledge of misconceptions and shown the generality and prevalence of many of these. It has provided convincing evidence that many learners fail to develop a sound, useable understanding of many fundamental scientific concepts and theoretical explanations. This, if we are genuinely interested in 'teaching for under-standing', is a major stimulus to change.

The influence on practice of research of this sort goes beyond the research findings themselves. The theoretical frameworks which under-pin research studies, and the analyses carried out in the course of research, can in themselves influence practices. So, for example, the ideas of Jean Piaget have been used to provide an explanation for some of the difficulties inherent in learning science, and to develop a taxonomy for estimating the 'cognitive demand' of different ideas (Shayer and Adey 1981). This in turn has led to specific suggestions for restructuring and re-sequencing curricula and teaching programmes. Another influential theoretical framework is the constructivist perspec-tive on learning: that learning involves the active 'construction of meaning' by the learner and is strongly influenced by the learner's current conceptions. This general viewpoint on learning may influence teachers' practices more than any specific research finding from the research programme which it has stimulated. As regards the teaching of specific topics, a careful analysis of content, carried out in the course of a research study, may indicate missing steps in a teaching sequence, or raise questions about the order in which ideas are introduced. It would then be perfectly rational to make changes in one's teaching approach in the light of this analysis, and this could clearly be said to be an 'improvement' even if there is no empirical evidence that it results in better student learning outcomes. It is simply more satisfying to teach a topic in an order that you see as logical and coherent, than one which you have come to regard as incoherent.

To what extent, then, can school science education in the UK (and elsewhere) currently be termed 'research informed' or 'research evidence-informed'? Certainly many teachers and others working in science education (such as textbook authors, examiners, providers of initial and in-service teacher education) are aware of the large body of research on learning in science referred to above. Comments of many of those who were interviewed or participated in focus groups in EPSE Project 4 (Chapter 8) showed that they knew of this work. None, however, referred to any specific piece of research, or research finding, to explain why they went about the teaching of any specific topic or idea in the way that they did. Perhaps a more significant channel of influence is through the teaching materials that are used. Many Project 4 respondents referred to this conduit, though often in very general and non-specific terms and without giving illustrative examples. The treatments of some conceptually demanding topics in some textbooks suggest the authors' awareness of specific research findings – reflected in the order in which ideas are introduced or the emphasis given to certain points. More commonly, however, as we have commented earlier, topics and ideas that research has shown to be difficult are glossed over quickly, and important linking ideas omitted.

In addition to its possible influence on the way in which *specific* topics or ideas are taught, research might also be seen as influencing science teachers' practices through their use of *general* teaching and learning strategies and approaches – practices of types B and C in Table 9.1 above. Several Project 4 respondents mentioned this, indicating that they believed their use of practical work, or of 'active learning' methods, was warranted by research which showed that these teaching approaches lead to better learning. None, however, mentioned any specific research studies or findings. Knowledge of specific research evidence did not appear to be the reason for practitioners' choices of general teaching strategies of this sort. Rather, ideas about the effectiveness of such strategies – including, perhaps, a sense that they are warranted by research – seem to have become an integral component of science teachers' professional knowledge – a taken-for-granted, perhaps even constitutive, element of what it means to be 'an effective science teacher' (Donnelly 1999b).

To summarise, then, many aspects of current science education practice might reasonably be claimed to be research evidence-informed, in the sense that general features of the design of teaching episodes are consistent with general perspectives or views that have arisen from research, or which are believed by many teachers to be supported by research. However, there is little evidence of the direct influence of specific research findings on specific teaching choices and decisions. Would science education practice be improved were it to become more research-evidence informed? We believe that it would – that there is a large body of evidence and ideas arising from research which, if applied more widely and systematically to practice, would lead to significantly improved learning outcomes. One very significant aspect of that improvement would stem from greater clarity about learning outcomes, and more explicit recognition of the relative difficulty of different 'bits' of learning. Ideas that are conceptually demanding, yet critical for understanding, are not sufficiently highlighted in the current curriculum, or in the teaching resources that support it, and differentiated from less demanding material. As we have already commented, it was striking that none of the schools involved in Project 2 could clearly identify where in their teaching programme they taught students the atomic/molecular model of chemical reactions, or explain how they measured attainment of the key learning objectives of this centrally important piece of science teaching. Similarly, several teachers involved in Project 1 commented that one of the basic ideas probed by a group of questions was not something they had previously emphasised – but they could now see that it was important.

Research on learners' understanding of basic ideas not only clarifies the teaching and learning agenda, but also suggests ways in which understanding might be 'measured'. Offering an operational definition of 'understanding', as the ability to answer a particular question (or set of questions) correctly or to carry out a particular task (or set of tasks) appropriately, is therefore a particularly powerful way of clarifying learning outcomes. It may also influence teachers' decisions about how to allocate time and resources (encouraging them to spend more on the ideas that are critical for progress in understanding), suggest teaching activities and strategies for tackling these difficult ideas, and provide exemplars which stimulate and enable the development of 'more of the same'. Indeed these were the central ideas behind EPSE Project 1.

Deciding which outcomes are of most value is, of course, a matter of judgement. Perhaps one reason why research and practitioner communities do not interact better is that they are often interested in somewhat different outcomes. For teachers, the emphasis is, understandably, on those measures on which their performance is judged: in England, national tests at age 11 and 14, and General Certificate of Secondary Education (GCSE) examinations at age 16; in the United States, the state tests associated with the No Child Left Behind Act.

Researchers have tended to focus on 'understanding' of basic ideas, rather than on broader measures of attainment in whole subjects – seeing basic ideas as more precisely measurable, of greater inherent value, and more durable (less subject to policy-driven change, or change in fashion). This was clearly a potential issue in EPSE Project 1, where teachers were provided with banks of questions designed to probe understanding of basic ideas. In interviews, however, it became clear that many teachers, whilst recognising the importance to their students of national tests, also valued understanding as a goal. Although they recognised that the EPSE diagnostic probes were distinctly different from the questions used in national tests, most argued that students who had a better understanding of fundamental ideas would also be better able to answer the external test questions. So teaching for understanding and teaching for examination success were not seen as conflicting. Even so, it may be important to recognise that research is not the disinterested, value-free, collection and analysis of data. The choice of research questions and instruments implicitly sets the agenda for 'what counts'.

Finally, if research can lead to improvements in the design of teaching interventions, how can this be facilitated? First, we should acknowledge that it is not surprising that few teachers can point to specific pieces of their teaching in which they knowingly draw on a specific research finding. The step from research findings to practical responses is far from trivial. Only in exceptional instances do practical implications simply 'emerge' from the findings of research. More often the step from findings to responses is like formulating a hypothesis – using creativity and imagination (and drawing on other kinds of knowledge and insight) to propose a set of actions that might lead to improved outcomes. The challenge which this poses is insufficiently recognised. Often the final paragraphs of research articles propose some practical 'implications' or responses to what has been found. These, however, are invariably based on professional wisdom; rarely have they been worked out in detail, let alone tried out and evaluated. A justifiable criticism of much science education research is that it identifies the problem and then stops. We will return to this issue in the next section of this chapter. Here, the point we want to make is that curriculum engineering – enabling research to have an impact on practice – involves research *and development*. Hitherto, development (the D in R&D) has been undervalued. Its critical importance needs to be more explicitly recognised, and the value of such work, and the intellectual challenge it poses, acknowledged as comparable with the research phase (Burkhardt and Schoenfeld 2003).

Our own work illustrates this general point. The development of three extensive banks of diagnostic questions in EPSE Project 1 involved detailed analysis of the content of each subject domain, and the drafting and redrafting of questions to maximise clarity, minimise ambiguity, and devise formats that could be easily used in classroom contexts. This took more time and effort than the subsequent research phase in which we looked at the influence of these resources on teachers' practices. The development involved collaboration between researchers and teachers, and extensive field testing. Both are essential. Indeed this may be where practitioners can make a particularly important and valuable input into the R&D process, to ensure that the artefacts developed embody practitioner knowledge as well as knowledge from research. In Project 2, the final versions of the teaching sequences were the product of a process of drafting and redrafting, where at all times the authors were working to achieve a range of aims: supporting students' learning, providing guidance to the teacher, and producing well-paced and motivating lessons. The researchers and teachers each brought a distinctive expertise to this process, the final products being of genuine co-authorship. In the area of science teaching and learning with which Project 3 was concerned, there is a major step between the determination of broad curriculum goals and their enactment by teachers in science classrooms. Research knowledge can never completely specify how such goals should be approached. Rather, teaching approaches have to be developed in collaboration with teachers, drawing on teachers' professional knowledge to develop lessons and materials which are accessible and engaging.

The challenge of development work – the considered and reflective appraisal and use of research findings and insights to create a new 'object' (a set of teaching materials or guidelines that can be implemented in the classroom) – contrasts with the view that research can be effectively disseminated through short, accessible digests of research findings, which 'busy practitioners' can read and be stimulated to act upon (for references to some examples of this approach, see Cordingley 2004: 86). Whilst condensed, jargon-light summaries of research projects may have a valuable role in raising practitioners' and policy-makers' awareness of specific research studies, and of research in general, they are unlikely to stimulate significant changes in practice. Contradictions were very apparent in the views we collected in Project 4 (Chapter 8): in interviews, several teachers asked for shorter and more accessible accounts of research but, when presented with such accounts in focus groups, many raised questions about the way the research was conducted, indicating that they would need to know much more before being persuaded to alter their practice. Our work in EPSE Projects 1, 2 and 3 convinces us that the effort involved in taking thoughtful and considered account of relevant research findings and insights, and integrating this with practitioner knowledge to produce teaching materials or guidelines that can be directly implemented, is essential if research findings are to have a significant impact on classroom practice. To refer to this as 'translation' of the research findings into materials seems to underplay the effort involved. For that reason we prefer to talk of 'creating' (or 'constructing') a new object or artefact – a research evidence-informed teaching intervention. A further challenge, highlighted by Project 3 but present also in Projects 1 and 2, is the development of teachers' capabilities and confidence in using different forms of pedagogy, which some of these teaching materials might require.

The role of research in justifying the use of a teaching intervention

We now turn to the role of research in providing evidence of the *outcomes* of a teaching intervention – of the extent to which it 'works'. Throughout this book we have termed interventions for which such evidence exists 'research evidence-based'. If a major achievement of science education research has been to improve significantly our understanding of the nature of learning in science and the barriers to learning, then a weakness is that this better understanding of 'the problem' has not been followed by a comparable programme to develop and evaluate possible solutions. Studies reporting on the outcomes of teaching interventions do, of course, appear regularly in the research literature. Some have been discussed in Chapter 5. But rarely is the intervention described sufficiently clearly, or made available as a 'package' that a teacher could take up should they wish. Often the learning objectives are insufficiently clear, or the measures used to assess learning outcomes unconvincing. And often the evaluation design does not control the effects of other variables which might account for the effects observed. As a result, there are few interventions for which one could reasonably claim that sound and convincing research evidence exists of the outcomes that can be expected from using them. It is therefore not surprising that very little of school science education practice in the UK (or elsewhere) could currently be termed 'research evidence-based'.

So let us consider what might be involved in producing research evidence that a teaching intervention for a specific topic leads to better learning outcomes than other ways of teaching the topic, which is strong enough to justify advising other teachers to adopt it. We will look in turn at each of the three areas of weakness identified above in published evaluations of content-specific teaching interventions.

Specifying the intervention

Any teaching intervention that is to be evaluated systematically must be able to be clearly and fully described. The intervention must exist as a 'package', as otherwise it is unclear what is being tested. This would include all the teaching materials, together with any guidelines on how they are meant to be used. If training on the use of the materials is provided, then this too is part of the 'package' whose outcomes are being evaluated. It may also be important, and is certainly almost always useful, for developers of an intervention to highlight its characteristic features – the things which make it different from other ways of approaching the same topic, or which are judged by the developers to be critical for a successful outcome. This might include stating clearly the theoretical principles or ideas on which it is based and explaining how these have been implemented with the chosen content, or stating the design criteria used in developing the intervention and the reasons for choosing these. Relating this need to specify an intervention clearly to the studies reported in earlier chapters, the interventions in EPSE Project 2 were fully documented, and included all the teaching materials required, with full notes on their intended use. Similarly the banks of diagnostic questions, with guidance on ways of using them, which formed the intervention in Project 1, and the lesson materials and guidance in the final phase of Project 3, existed as clear and delineated 'objects'.

Measuring learning outcomes

The second requirement is that the intended learning outcomes of the teaching intervention must be stated clearly. Moreover, if we want the intervention to be widely taken up, these need to command broad consensus; if they are rather esoteric, a study that claims to show how they can be attained will make little impression on practitioners, however well the research evaluation is designed. The learning outcomes should also be reasonably durable. If not, they may have ceased to be of interest by the time a research evaluation is complete. Listing learning objectives, however, is not enough. We also need to make clear exactly how we are going to measure the extent to which they have been attained. The outcome 'measure' is in effect an operational definition of the intended outcomes – greatly clarifying what these actually mean. As with the learning outcomes, the outcome measure needs to command broad consensus – to be seen generally by practitioners as a valid and reliable indicator, which can discriminate those who have reached the intended outcome from those who are still working towards it. Usually, indeed, we want the outcome measure to provide a scale – on which a higher score can safely be taken as indicating improved performance. Without clarity about learning outcomes, and agreement about a means of 'measuring' them, it is not possible to evaluate a teaching intervention rigorously, or to compare two or more interventions.

EPSE Project 1 (Chapter 3), however, shows that the development of sound outcome measures is a major undertaking – even when the topic or idea being probed is fairly clear and well-defined. Questions that probe understanding of the same basic idea are often answered quite differently by the same student. No single question therefore provides a safe measure of understanding; several are needed. To develop an outcome measure, careful pre-testing is then needed, to explore the validity and reliability of individual questions and the internal consistency of sets of questions. At present no generally accepted measure of understanding exists for any major science idea or topic, at any level. In EPSE Project 3, the difficulty of devising outcome measures for key ideas about science led to the decision to focus on identifying necessary features of pedagogy rather than factors that correlate with better learning outcomes.

Another reason why clarity about outcomes and outcome measures is critically important is that new teaching interventions in science (and we suspect in many subjects) are rarely proposed as a better means of achieving exactly the same outcome as the existing approach. Much more often, they are part of a wider argument about learning goals. The argument is that we should emphasise different aspects of a topic or subject, or give higher priority to certain outcomes, than at present. The new intervention is then proposed as a means of doing this. But this means that the new and old teaching interventions cannot be directly compared – as they do not have the same objectives. Any outcome measure will inevitably favour one or the other. The interventions developed and evaluated in EPSE Projects 1–3 all involved some attempt to modify learning objectives. In Projects 1 and 2, it is a shift away from an emphasis on factual recall towards 'understanding'. In Project 3, the nature of science teaching goals are more explicitly recognised to be additions to the current objectives. Because new interventions may have somewhat different objectives from the current intervention, it is all the more important that outcome measures are transparent, and open to scrutiny. Even then, to claim that one intervention is 'better' than another is a statement about values, and not just about evidence.

Research design

The debates of the past decade about the quality of educational research have focused very strongly on the issue of research design. Randomised controlled trials (RCTs) and design experiments have been advocated as ways of generating sound and persuasive knowledge that can inform and influence practice and policy. Our view, as the discussion above may have indicated, is that equal attention needs to be paid to the clarity and quality of outcome measures. That said, research design clearly determines the conclusions that can logically be drawn from a study and may significantly affect its influence on practice and policy. Several teachers interviewed in EPSE Project 4 mentioned research design as a factor they would take into account in judging how persuasive a research finding is – with some referring to the need for matched control groups when testing an intervention. This needs, however, to be set in context: few indicated that research evidence was a major influence on their choice of teaching interventions and approaches.

The research design which provides the strongest evidence of the effects of an intervention is the randomised controlled trial. EPSE Project 2 is the element of our work which came closest to this. It used an experimental design, comparing learning outcomes in classes using a research-informed teaching intervention with those in matched classes in the same schools using the school's usual intervention for the same topic. For practical reasons, it was not possible to allocate classes randomly to experimental and control groups. Indeed it was difficult enough, given the current pressures on teachers in schools in England, to obtain a sample of teachers willing to use the experimental intervention, without the extra hurdle of having to tell our volunteers that only a randomly selected 50 per cent of them would be allowed to do so. But we would readily concede that the conclusions drawn might have been stronger had random allocation been feasible. Similarly, a larger sample size would also have enabled us to draw firmer conclusions and suggest implications with greater confidence.

Our work has, however, made us question the value of RCTs for evaluating many kinds of educational intervention and the wisdom of seeing this as the principal route towards evidence-based practice (see, for example, the 'worked example' discussion in Chapter 5). In the case of simple interventions, such as reducing class size, the case for using a randomised controlled trial to evaluate the intervention before implementing it widely is strong, provided the intended outcomes are clearly stated, and an accepted method of measuring them is agreed. For complex interventions, such as teaching interventions for specific topics or ideas, the value of RCTs is less clear. First, complex interventions need, as we have discussed above, to be clearly and fully specified so that they can be implemented reasonably consistently. Even if this is achieved, however, it is still difficult to interpret the outcomes, as advocates of RCTs for complex interventions in medicine and in education acknowledge (Moore 2002). To illustrate the difficulties, imagine a group of educators trying to devise an intervention to improve the teaching and learning of a specific topic or idea, X. They already have research evidence that there is currently a problem with the teaching and learning of X, and they are agreed that X is worth teaching. This is very much the situation we ourselves were in as we developed the interventions for EPSE Projects 1, 2 and 3. To design a teaching intervention that might improve the teaching of X, the developers need to have an idea (or ideas) about what might work better – they need some general principles, perhaps drawn from research or from professional experience, which lead to specific design criteria or design features. To apply these general principles or design criteria to the teaching of X, the developers must then make many more decisions and choices, some of which involve knowledge of and about X. Whilst we might hope (and predict) that the resulting intervention will be better than that currently in use, we would be very unlikely to want to claim that it is the best intervention that could possibly be produced using the chosen principles or criteria. There are far too many choices and decisions involved to make this plausible; some of these, whilst seeming apparently trivial, may in fact have a significant bearing on the outcome. (There may be 'critical details' in a teaching intervention as Viennot (2003) argues.) This raises a serious question about how we can decide which interventions are worth evaluating systematically – 'worth' in the sense that the outcomes might lead to useful knowledge. Often, what we are really looking for, when we evaluate an intervention, is evidence that the design principles and criteria on which it is based are good ones. An RCT, however, can only provide compelling evidence about the effects (if any) of *the actual intervention* that is trialled. A single trial cannot provide conclusive evidence of the merits of the theoretical principles or design criteria on which an intervention is based. Several trials, of interventions based on the same design principles or criteria but with different content, would be needed to achieve this.

The search for 'designs' that work but which might have to be modified and adapted to fit specific contexts – rather than for specific interventions that will work better anywhere – is central to the notion of the design experiment. Gorard (2004) argues that:

> The main objective of a design experiment is to produce an artefact, intervention or initiative in the form of a workable design. The emphasis . . . is on a general solution that can be 'transported' to any working environment where others might determine the final product within their particular context.
>
> (p. 101)

The focus here is not on how things work and might be explained, but on producing and improving artefacts (in our case, teaching interventions) and finding out how they perform under different conditions. For example, we might want to know the circumstances under which an intervention is likely to work well, and those where it is not – and to understand how it might be modified to make it work better in these. Unlike a trial, the method does not necessarily involve a direct comparison with another intervention – though clearly there must be some sense of trying to improve on current interventions and hence at least an implicit comparative element. Although not described as a design experiment, the work of Linn and Songer (1991) on the teaching of elementary thermodynamics provides an example from science education. Over a period of years, they evaluated and successively improved a middle school teaching intervention to help students differentiate and understand the ideas of heat and temperature. They recorded a steady rise in the proportion of the cohort who met their 'strong criteria' for understanding the heat/temperature distinction, from 3 per cent to 49 per cent. The time sequence data also help to identify specific new activities, or features of the intervention, that correlate with larger increases in the proportion meeting this criterion and so might be responsible for causing these. Two major strengths of this work are the fact that the intervention is a clearly defined and delimited 'package', and the clarity and quality of the outcome measure (the criterion for judging a student to have understood the heat/temperature distinction). Clear success and failure criteria are essential if design experiments are to provide compelling grounds for recommending others to adopt a particular approach, or an intervention based upon it.

Relating these issues to our own work, the interventions developed in EPSE Project 2 (Chapter 5) were based on two main design considerations: giving a greater share of teaching time to the learning steps within the topic that previous research has shown to be particularly difficult, using activities designed to overcome those difficulties; and encouraging the use of dialogic and authoritative talk to support different teaching purposes in the intervention. The development phase of Project 2 could be seen as establishing 'proof of principle' for these interventions – using the outcomes of each school's normal teaching approach to the same topic as a baseline. The subsequent transfer phase then provided evidence that the same positive outcomes can be achieved more generally. The fact that similar outcomes were observed in two different science topic areas, using two different interventions based on the same design principles, strengthens the warrant for claiming that these outcomes can be attributed in part to the theoretical principles and design criteria that informed their design. As the sample is small, we cannot claim to know that the designed intervention will achieve better results than *all* schools' normal teaching approaches to this topic – a substantially wider and randomly selected sample would be needed to warrant such a claim. So whilst it would not be justified, on the basis of this study, to recommend that *all* schools adopt the Project 2 interventions in place of their current teaching approaches for these topics, it does provide grounds for asking teachers to consider whether their own practice is as effective and the warrant for adopting the approach they use. The research does not tell you what you should do, but it may tell you that you should look harder at what you currently do and ask if you can justify continuing to do it that way.

In a similar way, the final phase of EPSE Project 1 (Chapter 6) can be seen as establishing 'proof of principle' for the idea that provision of teaching materials of a certain structure and type can lead to changes in aspects of teachers' classroom practices and their students' responses and engagement. It does not show that these changes will invariably be obtained, but that they *can* be obtained – indeed that some are quite likely outcomes. This prepares the ground for a more tightly designed study of the impact of the provision of such resources on teachers' practices and students' learning. As similar effects on teachers' practices were found in several different topic areas, Project 1 also provides some evidence in support of the general principles that underlie the actual materials produced, and not just of the merits and effects of these specific teaching artefacts.

Impacting on practice

The teaching interventions we have been considering in this book have one important characteristic whose implications we have not yet discussed: they are of a scale and type that places them within a teacher's or a school department's area of discretion. Adopting them involves the sorts of choices that most teachers are able to make. They are unlikely to be imposed from above, but rather to be voluntarily adopted. The critical question for research, therefore, is not about the outcomes that are obtained when such interventions are imposed, but when they are freely chosen, by teachers who see in them something that is attractive or which they believe will improve matters in their own local context. The RCT design does not (normally) address this question. Rather it allocates teachers or classes randomly to the experimental or control condition. But imagine a situation in which a new intervention seems attractive to 50 per cent of teachers, but not to the other 50 per cent – and that both groups are correct in their view that they will achieve better outcomes if they use the intervention they prefer. (This is not far-fetched: the new intervention might, for example, emphasise student–student discussion and dialogue, whilst the current intervention uses more teacher-centred methods – and there is evidence that teachers differ widely in their ability and confidence to manage both methods effectively.) Random allocation will then result in a null outcome, as half of each sample will have been allocated to the intervention they do not like and with which they in fact achieve poorer results – cancelling out the improved outcomes obtained by the other half who are allocated to the intervention they prefer. If both groups were allowed to choose, both would obtain improved outcomes. This thought experiment shows the risk of false negatives – of potentially useful interventions being rejected. For advocates of RCTs, individual preferences are simply one factor (among many) that contributes to variation in outcomes, and can be taken care of by randomisation. Pawson and Tilley (1997) take a contrary view. They argue that:

> *choice is the very condition of social and individual change and not some kind of practical hindrance to understanding that change.* . . . it is not programmes [or interventions] which work, as such, but people co-operating and choosing to make them work.
>
> (p. 36, their emphases)

Whereas RCTs have a valuable role in evaluating any intervention that is to be compulsorily introduced – indeed we would argue that all such interventions *should* be evaluated in this way before being imposed – their role in evaluating teaching interventions that must compete in the 'marketplace', and are voluntarily adopted or neglected, is much less clear. Here the aim must surely be to produce the sort of evidence that those who make these choices see as useful, relevant and convincing. The practitioners we interviewed in EPSE Project 4 did not seem to be looking for, or even to believe in the existence of, interventions that invariably work better and should therefore be adopted, but rather for evidence that an intervention might work better for them, in the specific situation in which they find themselves. Evidence that an intervention works better 'on average' might therefore be rejected because of a professional judgement that the practitioner's own situation and context would be one of those where it worked less well. It is also possible that some teachers (or school departments) might consider themselves aware of the same issues and sources of design inspiration as the developers of an intervention that had been trialled, and had come up with (and were already using) a response that they preferred.

For these situations of professional choice, an R&D approach like that outlined by Burkhardt and Schoenfeld (2003) seems to offer a more viable way forward – in terms of both its practicability and its potential to stimulate changes in practice. The first step is to show that the intervention in which we are interested can achieve the desired outcomes in some situations at least (perhaps when used by one of its designers). The more clearly the 'success criteria' are stated, and the better the outcome measures used, the more persuasive this will be. The question of interest then is: in which situations, and under what conditions, can similar outcomes be obtained? The aim of research is not to show whether or not an intervention 'works better' in general. Rather it is to understand better the conditions under which it can achieve the outcomes we want – and perhaps also to understand how it achieves them. This does not mean that all we can ever say is that 'context matters'; depending on the scale and design of a research evaluation, either using RCT or design experiment methods, we may be able to provide strong evidence that a particular intervention merits serious consideration – or conversely that another (perhaps the one you are currently using) can no longer be defended as a rational choice.

We see evidence-based education (paraphrasing the extract from Sackett *et al.* (1996) cited in Chapter 1), as 'the conscientious, explicit and judicious use of current best evidence in making decisions about how to achieve specific educational goals' (p. 71). The kinds of goals we have focused on in this book are students' understanding of the ideas, concepts and skills that are of central importance for making progress in understanding of a subject. Sackett *et al.* are careful to make clear that they are not advocating 'cookbook' medicine, in which a doctor's decisions are effectively taken by the research evidence. Professional expertise has a crucial role in interpreting that evidence and deciding how best to deal with individual patients. In the same way, evidence-based practice in education does not, in our view, mean aiming to produce a collection of interventions that carry the label 'evidence-based practice' – which teachers should therefore adopt and use because research evidence shows that this will lead to the best overall outcome. Rather it would mean teachers exercising professional judgement about how best to undertake *specific* pieces of teaching *in their own work context*, drawing on the best available information about what has been found to work elsewhere. Two key words in the definition above are 'explicit' and 'judicious'. We need to work towards a situation in which research evidence is routinely an explicit input to teachers' decision making, but where it is also accepted that this must be weighed judiciously alongside other kinds of knowledge to reach a decision that can be rationally defended. This does not imply a diminution of the professional expertise of teachers, as some critics of the idea of evidence-based education seem to fear. Rather, being able to provide a rational account of the reasons for specific choices and decisions, based on research evidence, would, in our view, significantly enhance the standing of teaching as a profession.

Summary

In this concluding chapter, we begin by noting that there is a very wide range of types of educational action that might be termed a 'practice'. We argue that research has a clearer and more valuable role in the design of a teaching intervention, or in generating evidence of the effects of an intervention, if that intervention is relatively short, and has clear learning objectives whose attainment can be measured. Using research systematically in designing a teaching intervention will normally involve general design principles or criteria, applied within the context set by the chosen content. Its quality depends on both the general principles *and* how well they are implemented with this content. The learning outcomes observed

continued

similarly depend on both of these. Interventions that are adopted voluntarily rather than imposed may be better evaluated through research studies that do not ask if an intervention 'works', but rather if users are able to 'make it work' for them, in their context.

Outline summaries of the four projects undertaken by the Evidence-based Practice in Science Education (EPSE) Research Network

Project 1: Promoting diagnostic assessment

Background

Many researchers have used written and oral probes of students' ideas and reasoning about many aspects of the natural world, to document common misconceptions and 'alternative' (non-scientific) explanations of phenomena. Providing tools similar to those used by researchers, which enable teachers to collect focused diagnostic data quickly and easily in their own classes, may be a more powerful stimulus to change than reports of the findings of research conducted elsewhere. This might also encourage teachers make greater use of formative assessment ('assessment for learning'), which has been shown by several research studies to have a significant positive impact on student learning outcomes, and attitudes to learning.

Aims

- To develop banks of diagnostic questions, based on the kinds of probes used by researchers, that can be used by science teachers to monitor the development of students' understanding of some important science ideas and topics.
- To use a sample of these questions to evaluate students' understanding, at different ages, of a number of key ideas in some important science domains.
- To investigate the changes in teachers' practices which result from providing them with a bank of diagnostic questions, and the impact of this on student responses and learning.

What we did

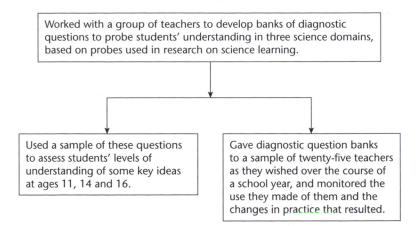

Worked with a group of teachers to develop banks of diagnostic questions to probe students' understanding in three science domains, based on probes used in research on science learning.

Used a sample of these questions to assess students' levels of understanding of some key ideas at ages 11, 14 and 16.

Gave diagnostic question banks to a sample of twenty-five teachers as they wished over the course of a school year, and monitored the use they made of them and the changes in practice that resulted.

Question banks were developed in collaboration with a group of practitioners. The group chose the science topics to work on: forces and motion, particle models of matter, and electric circuits. The development of questions involved collecting probes used in research on students' ideas about phenomena in these topic areas, and modifying these to improve clarity and ease of classroom use. These were then pilot tested with samples of students. The question banks, and the detailed analysis of content that informed their development and the order in which they are presented, are themselves important practical outcomes of the project.

Short tests of key ideas in all three topic areas, using a selection of these questions, were then given to samples of 200–250 students drawn from five schools, at each of three age points (11, 14 and 16 years). Based on other measures, the science performance of all of these samples was 0.5–1.0 s.d. above the national average for the age group. Responses were coded to identify common responses, and to explore the consistency with which explanations and models were used across question contexts.

The sample of teachers who used the diagnostic question banks were broadly representative of secondary teachers in England, as were their schools. All three main science subjects were represented, and the sample included teachers with a wide range of teaching experience. Outline suggestions on ways of using the questions were given, but no extended training was provided. In-depth interviews in the teachers' schools were used to collect data on their use of the question banks, and their views on them. This was augmented by some questionnaire data and samples of students' work.

Main findings

* Levels of understanding of many key ideas in these science topic areas are low, and some change little with age. Current teaching approaches in science appear not to lead to widespread under-standing of many core ideas – and current assessment practices do not highlight this as a cause for concern.
* Many students use different models to answer questions probing understanding of the same basic idea. Several questions are needed to provide sound evidence of an individual student's reasoning.
* Teachers' repertoire of teaching approaches for these topics was extended, often quite markedly, by having access to a question bank. Many used questions as stimuli for whole-class discussion; almost all reported an increased use of small-group discussion. Several who were teaching topics outside their main science specialism commented that the questions helped them to teach in ways they found more satisfying (with more interaction and better student engagement).
* Most teachers thought the questions provided them with useful information on individual students' understandings within the classroom context and in the course of normal work. All felt that students' understanding of key points had been enhanced. Many reported, somewhat to their surprise, that students were interested to discuss the quite abstract ideas which some questions probed, often at length.

Project 2: Designing and evaluating teaching interventions

Background

There is a very large body of research documenting students' ideas about many aspects of the natural world, which indicates that many have misconceptions about phenomena and explain these using ideas and forms of reasoning that differ from the accepted scientific ones. Although there is an assumption that using research evidence about students' understanding in the design of teaching is likely to result in improvements in learning outcomes, there is a very limited evidence base against which this assumption can be tested. Very few studies have been conducted which develop and evaluate teaching interventions that are designed explicitly to address learning difficulties that have been identified. We therefore know very little about how – and whether – evidence about students' ideas can be used by teachers in planning teaching which makes a positive, measurable impact on students' understanding of science.

Aims

- To evaluate whether short science teaching sequences, informed by research evidence, can be designed and implemented in such a way as to have a measurable impact on students' understanding of the target science content.
- To see whether any gains obtained by teachers involved in developing such teaching sequences can also be obtained by others who were not involved in their development.

What we did

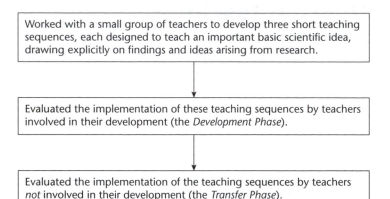

The three sequences, designed for use with students in the 11–15 age range and each lasting for no more than 6 hours, dealt with: the idea of electric current in simple circuits; basic ideas about plant nutrition, and modelling physical and chemical change in terms of a simple particle model.

Each of the nine *Development Phase* teachers taught the teaching sequence that they had worked on to at least one of their classes. Students completed tests, relating to the content of the teaching, both before and after the intervention. Similar data were collected in another class in the same school, of students judged by the school to be comparable, being taught the same part of the national curriculum. Comparisons were only made where pre-test data suggested that it was valid to do so. In addition, all the lessons were video-recorded using a static camera, with the teacher wearing a personal microphone. These data were used to evaluate the extent to which conceptual content and teacher talk in the lessons was consistent with the planned approach. Each teacher was also interviewed both before and after teaching, to ascertain their reactions to the teaching sequences and to explore reasons for any changes in approach.

During the *Transfer Phase* of the study, the biology and physics teaching sequences were taught by four biology teachers and five physics teachers who were not involved in their development. Data on students' learning and classroom interactions, similar to those collected in the *Development Phase*, were again collected. These were used to determine the extent to which learning gains noted in the *Development Phase* were replicated. As in the *Development Phase*, judgements were made about the extent to which the lessons were taught in a way consistent with their design intentions.

Main findings

- Teaching sequences which focused attention on ideas known from research to be difficult for many students, and which drew on both research and professional knowledge to devise activities to address these, resulted in improved attainment of conceptual goals when implemented by teachers involved in their design.
- Similar student learning gains were also obtained by teachers not involved in the design of the teaching sequences.
- Some of the teachers were able to implement the designers' intentions as regards matching of types of classroom discourse appropriately to tasks of different kinds.

Project 3: Teaching 'ideas about science'

Background

There is wide agreement that citizens need to know *about* science, in addition to having some scientific knowledge, in order to engage with issues and decisions that arise in everyday life. It is less clear exactly what should be taught, and how much agreement there is about this component of the curriculum. Teaching 'ideas about science' may also pose a significant challenge for teachers, and we therefore need to understand better the factors which facilitate or hinder this.

Aims

The original aims of the project were:

- To determine the extent of 'expert' consensus on what school students should be taught about scientific knowledge and the processes of scientific enquiry ('ideas about science'), and the student performances that would indicate attainment of the targets identified.
- To develop and evaluate teaching materials to improve students' understanding of the 'ideas about science' identified.

In the light of the outcomes of the first phase of the project and discussions with collaborating teachers, the second aim was modified and became:

- To identify the elements of effective practice in teaching 'ideas about science'.

What we did

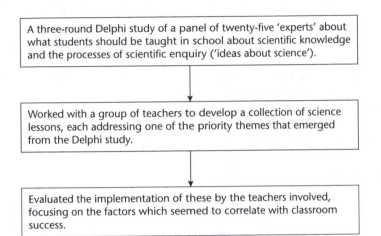

A three-round Delphi study of a panel of twenty-five 'experts' about what students should be taught in school about scientific knowledge and the processes of scientific enquiry ('ideas about science').

Worked with a group of teachers to develop a collection of science lessons, each addressing one of the priority themes that emerged from the Delphi study.

Evaluated the implementation of these by the teachers involved, focusing on the factors which seemed to correlate with classroom success.

Phase 1

The panel for the Delphi study consisted of twenty-three acknowledged experts on science communication, including: practising scientists; science teachers; science educators; historians, philosophers and sociologists of science; and people involved in the public understanding of science. Throughout, none was aware of the identities of the others. Responses to Round 1 were circulated anonymously to inform responses in Round 2, and a similar procedure was adopted for Round 3. Each round of questionnaire responses was coded by two members of the research team using the qualitative data analysis package (NUD*IST NVivo), and categories were amended to achieve a coding reliability above 80 per cent. The aim of this analysis was to identify the ideas or themes which the panel saw as of greatest importance, the extent of agreement about these, and any marked differences between sub-groups within the panel.

Phase 2

Three primary (age 8–11), four lower secondary (age 11–14) and four upper secondary (age 15–16) teachers were recruited to develop a range of strategies and materials for teaching the nine themes which emerged from the Delphi study. Six training days were used to develop these teachers' understanding of the themes, to develop teaching materials and strategies to address them, and to share their experiences of the variety of approaches they tried across a year long study. The research team visited each teacher in their school, and video-recorded two lessons that addressed the teaching of these themes. Field notes of lessons and teachers' meetings, instruments used to determine the teachers' views on the nature of science, and interviews conducted with the teachers before and after teaching the lessons provided additional data. The lessons were then summarised in a set of lesson transcripts and the data examined iteratively to search for the major themes and patterns that characterise effective teaching of 'ideas about science'.

Main findings

- There was a consensus amongst the 'experts' about nine common elements of 'ideas about science', or 'themes', that should be part of the school science curriculum.
- When teaching lessons addressing these themes, teachers' pedagogical style and views on teaching seemed to be at least as important as their understanding of the nature of science. In particular, teachers' ability to structure and facilitate more open dialogic questioning in the classroom was often of paramount importance to the success of the lesson.

Project 4: Exploring practitioners' views

Background

Calls for evidence-based practice raise issues about what constitutes 'evidence' for development of educational policy and classroom practice. Researchers have developed models of reflective practice and explored the use of tacit, professional knowledge by teachers. Less has been done to understand the nature and extent of use of research evidence by practitioners. The views of 'users' of research may help us to understand why some research findings and noted and perhaps acted on, while others are not. Practitioners' views of research may influence the approach they take to judging the effectiveness of their own practice, and evaluating the effects of any changes they make. An understanding of how practitioners see the nature and impact of research may also provide insights on the interface, and the channels of influence, between research and practice.

Aims

- To explore the views of science teachers, and other potential users of science education research, on the actual and potential impact of research on their everyday professional practices.
- To obtain a better understanding of the extent to which teachers and other user groups recognise and make use of research findings in the course of their normal practice.
- To explore the factors which promote and inhibit the impact of research in science education on practice.

What we did

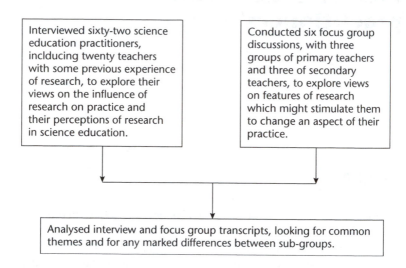

The interviews and focus group discussions were complementary in their objectives. Semi-structured interviews of 30–40 minutes duration were used to explore how individual practitioners viewed research processes and evidence. The first two questions sought interviewees' perceptions of the influence of research on their current practice. The third question explored participants' perceptions of the nature of educational research by asking them to sort a set of cards, describing examples of enquiry, into 'research' and 'not research' categories. Subsequent questions explored the sources to which interviewees thought they would look for ideas to improve their practice and the place of research among these, how they would evaluate a change in their practice, their views on the potential for research to improve science education, and the sources of their knowledge of research.

The focus groups examined the extent to which findings from science education research were seen as convincing and persuasive, and might lead to a change in practice. Each focus group had six to eight members and discussion lasted about 90 minutes. Focus group participants were presented in advance with eight vignettes summarising real examples of educational research. Discussion concentrated on the extent to which participants were familiar with the research described, found it credible or convincing, and their views on whether it might (or should) influence their practice. The aim was to establish teachers' perceptions of the extent to which research can provide general guidelines for practice, and their views on what counts as 'evidence' in relation to their everyday practice.

Transcripts of interviews and focus groups were analysed by scrutinising them iteratively to identify major emerging patterns and themes. The qualitative data software package (NUD*IST NVivo) was used to assist in the mechanics of coding and to help in identifying similarities and differences between the main sub-groups within the sample. Four researchers coded the transcripts, concentrating initially on data collected at their centre. Inter-researcher reliability was established through blind coding of several interviews. This indicated that 80 per cent of initial codes were being used in a consistent way across researchers; the use of codes with lower consistency was clarified by discussion and comparison of additional transcripts.

Main findings

- Many teachers see science education research as having an influence on their everyday practice.
- Examples of research influence given were predominantly of general, or indirect, influences on practice; few identified specific research influences on their teaching of particular topics, ideas or skills.
- Practice appears more likely to be altered by the uptake of research-informed teaching materials or practice guidelines than by reports of research findings.
- Many science teachers used quite stringent criteria when judging reports of research. Views on social research often seemed to draw on ideas about research methods and approaches in the natural sciences.
- Most teachers, however, said that they would use general measures of outcome, or rely on more qualitative evidence, to assess the impact of a change they had made in their practice. Few appeared to see this as 'research'.
- Research appears more likely to influence practice where there is a professional culture which encourages awareness of research and experimentation with practice. Professional networks which bring researchers and practitioners together were frequently mentioned as facilitating practitioners' awareness of research and making it more likely to influence their practice.

References

21st Century Science Project Team (2003) '21st Century Science – A new flexible model for GCSE science', *School Science Review*, 85 (310): 27–34.

AAAS (American Association for the Advancement of Science) (1993) *Benchmarks for Scientific Literacy*, Washington, DC: AAAS.

AAAS (American Association for the Advancement of Science) (1998) *Blueprints for Reform: Science, Mathematics and Technology Education*, New York: Oxford University Press.

Abd-El-Khalick, F. and Lederman, N.G. (2000) 'Improving science teachers' conceptions of the nature of science: A critical review of the literature', *International Journal of Science Education*, 22 (7): 665–702.

Adey, P. and Shayer, M. (1990) 'Accelerating the development of formal thinking in middle and high school pupils', *Journal of Research in Science Teaching*, 27 (3): 267–285.

Adey, P. and Shayer, M. (1993) 'An exploration of long-term transfer effects following an extended intervention programme in the high school science curriculum', *Cognition and Instruction*, 11 (1): 1–29.

Adey, P., Shayer, M. and Yates, C. (1996) *Thinking Science. The Materials of the CASE Project*, 2nd edn, Cheltenham: Nelson Thornes.

Aikenhead, G.S. (1987) 'High school graduates' beliefs about science-technology-society. III Characteristics and limitations of scientific knowledge', *Science Education*, 71 (4): 459–487.

Ajzen, I. and Fishbein, M. (1980) *Understanding Attitudes and Predicting Social Behaviour*, Englewood Cliffs, NJ: Prentice Hall.

Alexander, R. (2004) *Towards Dialogic Teaching*, York: Dialogos.

Alters, B.J. (1997) 'Whose nature of science?' *Journal of Research in Science Teaching*, 34 (1): 39–55.

Atkinson, P. and Delamont, S. (1977) 'Mock-ups and cock-ups: The stage management of guided discovery instruction', in P. Woods and M. Hammersley (eds) *School Experience: Explorations in the Sociology of Education*, London: Croom Helm.

Ausubel, D.P. (1968) *Educational Psychology: A Cognitive View*, New York: Holt, Rinehart and Winston.

Bain, A. (1879) *Education as a Science*, London: Kegan Paul. (Cited in J. Nisbet (1980) 'Educational research: The state of the art', in W.B. Dockrell and D. Hamilton (eds) *Rethinking Educational Research*, London: Hodder and Stoughton.)

Bakhtin, M.M. (1934) 'Discourse in the Novel', in M. Holquist (ed.) (1981) *Bakhtin, M.M. The Dialogic Imagination*, trans. C. Emerson and M. Holquist, Austin, TX: University of Texas Press.

Barnes, D. (1976) *From Communication to Curriculum*, Harmondsworth: Penguin Books.

Barnett, J. and Hodson, D. (2001) 'Pedagogical context knowledge: Toward a fuller understanding of what good science teachers know', *Science Education*, 85 (4): 426–453.

Bartholomew, H., Osborne, J. and Ratcliffe, M. (2004). 'Teaching students "ideas about science": Five dimensions of effective practice', *Science Education*, 88 (5): 655–682.

Bell, B. (1984) *Aspects of Secondary Students' Understanding of Plant Nutrition: Summary Report*, Leeds: Centre for Studies in Science and Mathematics Education, University of Leeds.

Black, P. and Wiliam, D. (1998a) 'Assessment and classroom learning', *Assessment in Education*, 5 (1): 7–74.

Black, P. and Wiliam, D. (1998b) *Inside the Black Box: Raising Standards through Classroom Assessment*, London: School of Education, King's College.

Blunkett, D. (2000) 'Influence or irrelevance: Can social science improve government?' *Research Intelligence*, 71: 12–21.

Bond, T.G. and Fox, C.M. (2001) *Applying the Rasch Model. Fundamental Measurement in the Human Sciences*, Mahwah, NJ: Lawrence Erlbaum.

Boruch, R. (1997) *Randomised Controlled Experiments for Planning and Evaluation: A Practical Guide*, Thousand Oaks, CA: Sage.

Brickhouse, N. (1991) 'Teachers' beliefs about the nature of science and their relationship to classroom practice', *Journal of Teacher Education*, 41 (3): 53–62.

Brickhouse, N.W., Dagher, Z.R., Letts IV, W.J. and Shipman, H.L. (2000) 'Diversity of students' views about evidence, theory and the interface between science and religion in an astronomy course', *Journal of Research in Science Teaching*, 37 (4): 340–362.

Brooks, V. (2002) *Assessment in Secondary Schools*, Buckingham: Open University Press.

Brown, A. (1992) 'Design experiments: Theoretical and methodological challenges in creating complex interventions in classroom settings', *Journal of the Learning Sciences*, 2 (2): 141–178.

Brown, D. and Clement, J. (1991), 'Classroom teaching experiments in mechanics', in R. Duit, F. Goldberg and H. Niedderer (eds) *Research in Physics Learning: Theoretical and Empirical Studies*, Kiel, Germany: Institüt für die Pädagogik der Naturwissenschaften (IPN).

Brown. S. and McIntyre, D. (1993) *Making Sense of Teaching*, Buckingham: Open University Press.

Burkhardt, H. and Schoenfeld, A.H. (2003) 'Improving educational research: Toward a more useful, more influential, and better-funded enterprise', *Educational Researcher*, 32 (9): 3–14.

Bybee, R. (1997) *Achieving Scientific Literacy: From Purposes to Practical Action*, Portsmouth, NH: Heinemann.

Campbell, M., Fitzpatrick, R., Haines, A., Kinmonth, A.L., Sandercock, P., Spiegelhalter, D. and Tyrer, P. (2000) 'Framework for design and evaluation of complex interventions to improve health', *British Medical Journal*, 321: 694–696.

Charis Project (2000) *Charis Science. Units (11–14)*, Nottingham: The Stapleford Centre.

Chi, M.T.H. (1992) 'Conceptual change within and across ontological categories: Examples from learning and discovery in science', in R. Giere (ed.) *Cognitive Models of Science: Minnesota Studies in the Philosophy of Science*, Minneapolis, MN: University of Minnesota Press.

Cochran, S.W. (1983) 'The Delphi method: Formulating and refining group judgements', *Journal of the Human Sciences*, 2: 111–117.

Collins, A. (1993) 'Toward a design science of education', in E. Scanlon and T. O'Shea (eds) *New Directions in Educational Technology*, New York: Springer Verlag.

Collins, H. and Pinch, T. (1993) *The Golem: What Everyone Should Know About Science*, Cambridge: Cambridge University Press.

Cordingley, P. (1999) 'Constructing and critiquing reflective practice', *Educational Action Research*, 7 (2): 183–190.

Cordingley, P. (2004) 'Teachers using evidence: Using what we know about teaching and learning to reconceptualize evidence-based practice', in R. Pring and G. Thomas (eds) *Evidence-Based Practice in Education*, Maidenhead: Open University Press.

Costa, N., Marques, L. and Kempa, R. (2000) 'Science teachers' awareness of findings from education research', *Research in Science and Technological Education*, 18 (1): 37–44.

Cotham, J.C. (1979) 'The development, validation and application of an instrument to assess teachers' understanding of philosophic aspects of scientific theories', unpublished Ph.D. thesis, Michigan State University.

Darling-Hammond, L. and Youngs, P. (2002) 'Defining "highly qualified teachers": What does "scientifically-based research" actually tell us?' *Educational Researcher*, 31 (9): 13–25.

Davies, H.T.O., Nutley S.M. and Smith, P.C. (eds) (2000) *What Works? Evidence-based Policy and Practice in Public Services*, Bristol: The Policy Press.

Davies, P. (1999) 'What is evidence-based education?' *British Journal of Educational Studies*, 47 (2): 108–121.

Day, C. (1999) 'Researching teaching through reflective practice', in J. Loughran (ed.) *Researching Teaching: Methodologies and Practices for Understanding Pedagogy*, London: Falmer Press.

Delbecq, A.L., Van de Ven, A.H. and Gustafson, D.H. (1975) *Group Techniques for Program Planning*, Glenview, IL: Scott Foreman.

DES (Department of Education and Science) (1989) *Science in the National Curriculum*, London: HMSO.

Désautels, J. and Larochelle, M. (1998) 'The epistemology of students: The "thingified" nature of scientific knowledge', in B. Frazer and K. Tobin (eds) *International Handbook of Science Education*, Dordrecht, Netherlands: Kluwer.

DETYA (Department of Education, Training and Youth Affairs) (2001) *Educational Research: In whose interests?* Higher Education Series Report no. 39, Canberra: DETYA Higher Education Division.

DfEE/QCA (Department for Education and Employment/Qualifications and Curriculum Authority) (1999) *Science. The National Curriculum for England*, London: DfEE.

DfES (Department for Education and Skills) (2002) *Key Stage 3 National Strategy. Framework for Teaching Science: Years 7, 8 and 9*, London: DfES.

Donnelly, J. (1999a) 'Schooling Heidegger. On being in teaching', *Teaching and Teacher Education*, 15: 933–949.

Donnelly, J. (1999b) 'Interpreting differences: the educational aims of teachers of science and history, and their implications', *Journal of Curriculum Studies*, 31(1): 17–41.

Doyle, C.S. (1993) 'The Delphi Method as a qualitative assessment tool for development of outcome measures for information literacy', *School Library Media Annual*, 11: 132–144.

Doyle, W. and Ponder, G. (1977–8) 'The practicality ethic in teacher decision making', *Interchange*, 8 (3), 1–12.

Driver, R., Squires, A., Rushworth, P. and Wood-Robinson, V. (1994) *Making Sense of Secondary Science: Research into Children's Ideas*, London: Routledge.

Driver, R., Leach, J., Millar, R. and Scott, P. (1996) *Young People's Images of Science*, Buckingham: Open University Press.

Duit, R. (2006) *Bibliography – Students' and Teachers' Conceptions and Science Education*, Kiel, Germany: Institüt für die Pädagogik der Naturwissenschaften (IPN). Online. Available HTTP: <http://www.ipn.uni-kiel.de/aktuell/stcse/stcse.html> (accessed 9 May 2006).

Duit, R. and Treagust, D. (1998) 'Learning in science – From behaviourism towards social constructivism and beyond', in B.J. Fraser and K.G. Tobin (eds) *International Handbook of Science Education*, Dordrecht, Netherlands: Kluwer.

Duschl, R.A. and Wright, E. (1989) 'A case study of high school teachers' decision making models for planning and teaching science', *Journal of Research in Science Teaching*, 26 (6): 467–501.

Ebel, R.L. and Frisbie, P.A. (1991) *Essentials of Educational Measurement*, Englewood Cliffs, NJ: Prentice Hall.

Edwards, T. (1996) 'The research base of effective teacher education', *Research Intelligence*, 57: 7–12.

Elliott, J. (2000) 'How do teachers define what counts as "credible evidence"? Some reflections based on interviews with teachers involved in the Norwich Area Research Consortium', paper presented at the British Educational Research Association Annual Conference, Cardiff University, September.

Engel Clough, E. and Driver, R. (1986) 'A study of consistency in the use of students' conceptual frameworks across different task contexts', *Science Education*, 70 (4): 473–496.

Enger, S.K. and Yager, R.E. (1998) *The Iowa Assessment Handbook*, University of Iowa: Science Education Center.

Enger, S.K. and Yager, R.E. (2001) *Assessing Student Understanding in Science*, Thousand Oaks, CA: Corwin Press.

Feasey, R. (ed.) (2001) *Science Is like a Tub of Ice Cream: Cool and Fun*, Hatfield: Association for Science Education.

Finegold, M. and Gorsky, P. (1991) 'Students' concepts of force as applied to related physical systems: A search for consistency', *International Journal of Science Education*, 13 (2): 97–113.

Fitz-Gibbon, C.T. (2000) 'Education: Realising the potential', in H.T.O. Davies, S.M. Nutley and P.C. Smith (eds) *What Works? Evidence-based Policy and Practice in Public Services*, Bristol: The Policy Press.

Frodeman, R. (2003) *Geo-Logic*, Albany, NY: State University of New York Press.

Fullan, M. (1991) *The New Meaning of Educational Change*, London: Cassell.

Fuller, S. (1997) *Science*, Buckingham: Open University Press.

Gallagher, J.J. (1991) 'Prospective and practicing secondary school science teachers' knowledge and beliefs about the philosophy of science', *Science Education*, 75 (1): 121–133.

Galton, M. (2000) 'Integrating theory and practice: Teachers' perspectives on educational research', paper presented at ESRC Teaching and Learning Research Programme Conference, University of Leicester, November.

Glynn, S, Duit, R. and Thiele, R. (1995) 'Teaching science with analogies: A strategy for constructing knowledge', in S.M. Glynn and R. Duit (eds) *Learning Science in the Schools: Research Reforming Practice*, Mahwah, NJ: Lawrence Erlbaum.

Goldsworthy, A., Watson, R., and Wood-Robinson, V. (2000) *Developing Understanding in Scientific Enquiry*, Hatfield: Association for Science Education.

Goodrum, D., Hackling, M. and Rennie, L. (2001) *The Status and Quality of Teaching and Learning of Science in Australian Schools*, Canberra: Department of Education, Training and Youth Affairs.

Gorard, S. (2004) *Combining Methods in Educational and Social Research*, Maidenhead: Open University Press.

Gould, S.J. (1991) *Wonderful Life. The Burgess Shale and the Nature of History*, Harmondsworth, Penguin Books.

Gray, J. (1996) 'Track record of peer review: A reply to some remarks by David Hargreaves', *Research Intelligence*, 57: 5–6.

Gray, J.A.M. (2002) *Evidence-based Healthcare*, 2nd edn, Edinburgh: Churchill Livingstone.

Hacker, R.G. and Rowe, M.J. (1985) 'A study of teaching and learning processes in integrated science classrooms', *European Journal of Science Education*, 7 (2): 173–180.

Hammersley, M. (1997) 'Educational research and teaching: A response to David Hargreaves' TTA lecture', *British Educational Research Journal*, 23 (2): 141–161.

Hargreaves, D.H. (1996) *Teaching as a Research-based Profession: Possibilities and Prospects* (Annual Lecture), London: Teacher Training Agency.

Harland, J. and Kinder, K. (1997) 'Teachers' Continuing Professional Development: Framing a model of outcomes', *British Journal of In-service Education*, 23 (1): 71–84.

Harlen, W. and Holroyd, C. (1997) 'Primary teachers' understanding of concepts of science: Impact on confidence and teaching', *International Journal of Science Education*, 19 (1): 93–105.

Harlen, W., Gipps, C., Broadfoot, P. and Nuttall, D. (1994) 'Assessment and the improvement of education', in B. Moon and A. Shelton-Mayes (eds) *Teaching and Learning in the Secondary School*, Buckingham: Open University Press.

Häussler, P., Frey, K., Hoffman, L., Rost, J. and Spada, H. (1980) *Education in Physics for Today and Tomorrow*, Kiel, Germany: Institüt für die Pädagogik der Naturwissenschaften (IPN).

Heslop, N., Brodie, D. and Williams, J. (2000) *Hodder Science – Pupils' Books and Teachers' Resource*, London: Hodder and Stoughton.

Hestenes, D., Wells, M. and Swackhamer, G. (1992) 'Force Concept Inventory', *The Physics Teacher*, 30: 141–157.

Hillage, J., Pearson, R., Anderson, A. and Tamkin, P. (1998) *Excellence in Research on Schools*, London: Department for Education and Employment.

Hodson, D. (1993) 'Philosophic stance of secondary school science teachers, curriculum experiences, and children's understanding of science', *Interchange*, 24 (1&2): 41–52.

Holquist, M. (1981) *Bakhtin, M.M. The Dialogic Imagination*, Austin, TX: University of Texas Press.

Huberman, M. (1993) 'The model of an independent artisan in teachers' professional relations', in J. Little and M. McLaughlin (eds) *Teachers' Work*, New York: Teachers College Press.

Jenkins, E. (1999) 'School science, citizenship and the public understanding of science', *International Journal of Science Education*, 21 (7): 703–710.

Johnson, P. (2000) 'Children's understanding of substances, Part 1: Recognising chemical change', *International Journal of Science Education*, 22 (7): 719–737.

Judd, R.C. (1971). 'Delphi decision methods in Higher Education administration', paper presented at the 12th American Meeting of the Institute of Management Sciences, Detroit.

Kennedy, M.M. (1997) 'The connection between research and practice', *Educational Researcher*, 26 (7): 4–12.

Kesidou, S. and Roseman, J.E. (2002) 'How well do middle school science programs measure up? Findings from Project 2061's curriculum review', *Journal of Research in Science Teaching*, 39 (6): 522–549.

Kouladis, V. and Ogborn, J. (1989) 'Philosophy of science: An empirical study of teachers' views', *International Journal of Science Education*, 11 (2): 173–184.

Labinger, J.A. and Collins, H. (eds) (2001) *The One Culture?* Chicago: University of Chicago Press.

Lakin, S. and Wellington, J. (1994) 'Who will teach the "nature of science"?: Teachers' views of science and their implications for science education', *International Journal of Science Education*, 16 (2): 175–190.

Latour, B. and Woolgar, S. (1986) *Laboratory Life: The Construction of Scientific Facts*, 2nd edn, Princeton, NJ: Princeton University Press.

Laudan, L. (1990) *Science and Relativism: Some Key Controversies in the Philosophy of Science*, Chicago: University of Chicago Press.

Leach, J. and Scott, P. (1995) 'The demands of learning science concepts: Issues of theory and practice', *School Science Review*, 76 (277): 47–52.

Leach, J. and Scott, P. (2002) 'Designing and evaluating science teaching sequences: An approach drawing upon the concept of learning demand and a social constructivist perspective on learning', *Studies in Science Education*, 38: 115–142.

Leach, J., Driver, R., Scott, P. and Wood-Robinson, C. (1996) 'Children's ideas about ecology 2: Ideas about the cycling of matter found in children aged 5–16', *International Journal of Science Education*, 18 (1): 19–34.

Leach, J., Hind, A. and Ryder, J. (2003) 'Designing and evaluating short teaching interventions about the epistemology of science in high school classrooms', *Science Education*, 87 (6): 831–848.

Lederman, N.G. (1992) 'Students' and teachers' conceptions of the nature of science: A review of the research', *Journal of Research in Science Teaching*, 29 (4): 331–359.

Lederman, N.G. and Abd-El-Khalick, F. (1998) 'Avoiding the de-natured science: Activities that promote understandings of the nature of science', in W.F. McComas (ed.) *The Nature of Science in Science Education: Rationales and Strategies*, Dordrecht, Netherlands: Kluwer.

Lederman, N.G. and O'Malley, M. (1990) 'Students' perceptions of the tentativeness in science: Development, use and sources of change', *Science Education*, 74 (2): 225–239.

Lemke, J.L. (1990) *Talking Science: Language, Learning and Values*, Norwood, NJ: Ablex Publishing Corporation.

Linn, M.C. and Songer, N. (1991) 'Teaching thermodynamics to middle school students: What are the appropriate cognitive demands?', *Journal of Research in Science Teaching*, 28 (10): 885–918.

Longino, H. (1990) *Science as Social Knowledge*, Princeton, NJ: Princeton University Press.

Loughran, J. (ed.) (1999) *Researching Teaching. Methodologies and Practices for Understanding Pedagogy*, London: Falmer Press.

Martorella, P. (1991) 'Consensus building among social educators: A Delphi study', *Theory and Research in Social Education*, 19 (1): 83–94.

Marx, R.W., Freeman, J.G., Krajcik, J.S. and Blumenfeld, P.C. (1998) 'Professional development of science teachers', in B.J. Fraser and K.G. Tobin (eds) *International Handbook of Science Education*, Dordrecht, Netherlands: Kluwer.

Matthews, M. (1995) *Constructivism and New Zealand Science Education*, Auckland: Dunmore Press.

Matthews, M. (1997) 'Introductory comments on philosophy and constructivism in science education', *Science & Education*, 6 (1): 5–14.

McNamara, O. (ed.) (2002) *Becoming an Evidence-based Practitioner: A Framework for Teacher-Researchers*, London: RoutledgeFalmer.

Mazur, E. (1997) *Peer Instruction*, New York: Prentice Hall.

Mellado, V. (1998) 'Preservice teachers' classroom practice and their conceptions of the nature of science', in B.J. Fraser and K.G. Tobin (eds) *International Handbook of Science Education*, Dordrecht, Netherlands: Kluwer.

Mercer, N. (2000) *Words and Minds: How We Use Language to Think Together*, London: Routledge.

Mercer, N. and Wegerif, R. (1998) 'Is "exploratory talk" productive talk?', in K. Littleton and P. Light (eds) *Learning with Computers. Analysing Productive Interaction*, London: Routledge.

Millar, R. (1996) 'Towards a science curriculum for public understanding', *School Science Review*, 77 (280): 7–18.

Millar, R. and Hunt, A. (2002) 'Science for Public Understanding. A different way to teach and learn science', *School Science Review*, 83 (304): 35–42.

Millar, R. and Osborne, J. (1998) *Beyond 2000. Science Education for the Future*, London: School of Education, King's College.

Moore, L. (2002) 'Research design for the rigorous evaluation of complex educational interventions: Lessons from health services research', *Building Research Capacity*, 1: 4–5.

Mortimer, E.F. (1998) 'Multivoicedness and univocality in the classroom discourse: An example from theory of matter', *International Journal of Science Education*, 20 (1): 67–82.

Mortimer, E.F. and Scott, P.H. (2003) *Meaning Making in Secondary Science Classrooms*, Buckingham: Open University Press.

Mosteller, F. and Boruch, R. (eds) (2002) *Evidence Matters: Randomized Trials in Education Research*, Washington, DC: Brookings Institution Press.

National Research Council (1995) *National Science Education Standards*, Washington, DC: National Academy Press.

Naylor, S. and Keogh, B. (2000) *Concept Cartoons in Education*, Sandbach: Millgate House Publishers.

Norris, N. (1996) 'Professor Hargreaves, the TTA and evidence-based practice', *Research Intelligence*, 57: 2–4.

Norris, S. and Phillips, L. (1994) 'Interpreting pragmatic meaning when reading popular reports of science', *Journal of Research in Science Teaching*, 31 (9): 947–967.

Ogborn, J., Kress, G., Martins, I. and McGillicuddy, K. (1996) *Explaining Science in the Classroom*, Buckingham: Open University Press.

Osborne, J.F. (1996) 'Beyond Constructivism', *Science Education*, 80 (1): 53–82.

Osborne, J.F. and Ratcliffe, M. (2001) *Developing Assessment Methods. Keeping National Curriculum Science in Step with the Changing World of the 21st Century*, report for the Qualifications and Curriculum Authority, Southampton/London: University of Southampton/King's College.

Osborne, J.F. and Ratcliffe, M. (2002) 'Developing effective methods of assessing Ideas-and-Evidence', *School Science Review*, 83 (305): 113–123.

Osborne, J.F., Ratcliffe, M., Collins, S., Millar, R. and Duschl, R. (2003) 'What "ideas about science" should be taught in school science? A Delphi study of the "expert" community', *Journal of Research in Science Teaching*, 40 (7): 692–720.

Palmer, D.H. (1998) 'Measuring contextual error in the diagnosis of alternative conceptions in science', *Issues in Educational Research*, 8 (1): 65–76.

Parlett, M. and Hamilton, D. (1972) *Evaluation as Illumination: A New Approach to the Study of Innovative Programmes*, Occasional Paper No. 9, Edinburgh: Centre for Research in the Educational Sciences, University of Edinburgh. (Reprinted in D. Tawney (ed.) (1976) *Curriculum Evaluation Today: Trends and Implications*, London: Macmillan.)

Pawson, R. and Tilley, N. (1997) *Realistic Evaluation*, London: Sage.

Psillos, D. (1998) 'Teaching Introductory Electricity', in A. Tiberghien, E.L. Jossem and J. Barojas (eds) *Connecting Research in Physics Education with Teacher Education*, International Commission on Physics Education. Online. Available HTTP: <http://www.physics.ohio-state.edu/~jossem/ICPE/TOC.html> (accessed 8 March 2005).

QCA (Qualifications and Curriculum Authority) (2000) *Science: A Scheme of Work for Key Stage 3*, London: QCA.

Ratcliffe, M. (1999) 'Evaluation of abilities in interpreting media reports of scientific research', *International Journal of Science Education*, 21 (10): 1085–1099.

Ratcliffe, M., Bartholomew, H., Hames, V., Hind, A., Leach, J., Millar, R. and Osborne, J. (2004) *Science Education Practitioners' Views of Research and its Influence on their Practice*, EPSE Research Report, York: Department of Educational Studies, University of York. Also Online. Available HTTP: <http://www.york.ac.uk/depts/educ/projs/EPSE> (accessed 8 March 2005).

Ratcliffe, M., Bartholomew, H., Hames, V., Hind, A., Leach, J., Millar, R. and

Osborne, J. (2005) 'Evidence-based practice in science education: The researcher–user interface', *Research Papers in Education*, 20 (2): 169–186.

Redish, E. (2003) *Teaching Physics with the Physics Suite*, New York: Wiley.

Rojas-Drummond, S. and Mercer, N. (2004) 'Scaffolding the development of effective collaboration and learning', *International Journal of Educational Research*, 39: 99–111.

Rudolph, J.L. (2000) 'Reconsidering the "nature of science" as a curriculum component', *Journal of Curriculum Studies*, 32 (3): 403–419.

Ryder, J. (2001) 'Identifying science understanding for functional scientific literacy', *Studies in Science Education*, 36: 1–44.

Sackett, D.L., Rosenberg, W.M.C., Gray, J.A.M., Haynes, R.B. and Richardson, W.S. (1996) 'Evidence-based medicine: What it is and what it isn't', *British Medical Journal*, 312: 71–72.

Sadler, P.M. (1998) 'Psychometric models of student conceptions in science: Reconciling qualitative studies and distractor-driven assessment instruments', *Journal of Research in Science Teaching*, 35 (3): 265–296.

Satterly, D. (1981) *Assessment in Schools*, Oxford: Blackwell.

Schwedes, H. and Dudeck, W.-G. (1996) 'Teaching electricity by help of a water analogy (how to cope with the need for conceptual change)', in G. Welford, J. Osborne and P. Scott (eds) *Research in Science Education in Europe*, London: Falmer Press.

Shavelson, R. and Towne, L. (eds) (2002) *Scientific Research in Education*, Washington, DC: National Academy Press.

Shayer, M. and Adey, P. (1981) *Towards a Science of Science Teaching*, London: Heinemann.

Shipstone, D.M. (1988) 'Students' understanding of simple electrical circuits', *Physics Education*, 23 (2): 92–96.

Shkedi, A. (1998) 'Teachers' attitudes towards research: A challenge for qualitative researchers', *International Journal of Qualitative Studies in Education*, 11 (4): 559–77.

Shulman, L.S. (1986) 'Those who understand: Knowledge growth in teaching', *Educational Researcher*, 15 (2): 4–14.

Shulman, L.S. (1987) 'Knowledge and teaching: Foundations of the new reform', *Harvard Educational Review*, 57 (1): 1–22.

Slavin, R.E. (2002) 'Evidence-based education policies: Transforming educational practice and research', *Educational Researcher*, 31 (7): 15–21.

Smith, K.S. and Simpson, R.D. (1995) 'Validating teacher competencies for faculty members in Higher Education: A national study using a Delphi study method', *Innovative Higher Education*, 19 (3): 223–234.

Stanley, W.B. and Brickhouse, N. (2001) 'Teaching sciences: The multicultural question revisited', *Science Education*, 85 (1): 35–49.

Stavy, R. and Tirosh, D. (2000) *How Students (Mis-)Understand Science and Mathematics: Intuitive Rules*, New York: Teachers College Press.

Sutton, C. (1995) 'The Scientific Model as a Form of Speech', in G. Welford,

J. Osborne and P. Scott (eds) *Research in Science Education in Europe*, London: Falmer Press.

Taylor, C.A. (1996) *Defining Science: A Rhetoric of Demarcation*, Madison, WI: University of Wisconsin Press.

Taylor, C. (2002) *The RCBN Consultation Exercise: Stakeholder Report*, Occasional Paper Series, no. 50, ESRC TLRP Research Capacity Building Network, Cardiff: Cardiff University.

Thompson, C.L. and Zeuli, J.S. (1999) 'The frame and the tapestry', in L. Darling-Hammond and G. Sykes (eds) *Teaching as the Learning Profession: Handbook of Policy and Practice*, San Francisco: Jossey-Bass.

Tiberghien, A. (1996) 'Construction of prototypical situations in teaching the concept of energy', in G. Welford, J. Osborne and P. Scott (eds) *Science Education Research in Europe: Current Issues and Themes*, London: Falmer Press.

Tiberghien, A. (2000) 'Designing teaching situations in the secondary school', in R. Millar, J. Leach, and J. Osborne, (eds) *Improving Science Education: The Contribution of Research*, Buckingham: Open University Press.

Tobin, K. and Tippins, D. (1993) 'Constructivism as a referent for teaching and learning', in K. Tobin (ed.) *The Practice of Constructivism in Science Education*, Washington, DC: AAAS Press.

Tooley, J. and Darby, D. (1998) *Educational Research: A Critique*, London: Office for Standards in Education (OfSTED).

Torgerson, C. and Torgerson, D. (2001) 'The need for randomized controlled trials in educational research', *British Journal of Educational Studies*, 49 (3): 316–328.

Treagust, D. (1988) 'Development and use of diagnostic tests to evaluate students' misconceptions in science', *International Journal of Science Education*, 10 (2): 159–169.

Turner-Bissett, R. (1999) 'The knowledge bases of the expert teacher', *British Educational Research Journal*, 25 (1): 39–55.

Tymms, P. and Fitz-Gibbon, C.T. (2002) 'Theories, hypotheses, hunches and ignorance', *Building Research Capacity*, 2: 10–11.

Tytler, R., Duggan, S. and Gott, R. (2001) 'Dimensions of evidence, the public understanding of science and science education', *International Journal of Science Education*, 23 (8): 815–832.

US Congress (2001) *No Child Left Behind Act of 2001*, Washington, DC: US Congress. Online. Available HTTP: <http://www.ed.gov/policy/elsec/leg/esea02/107-110.pdf> (accessed 10 February 2005).

US Department of Education (2002) *Strategic Plan 2002–2007*, Washington, DC: US Department of Education. Online. Available HTTP: <http://www.ed.gov/about/reports/strat/plan2002-07/plan.pdf> (accessed 10 February 2005).

US Department of Education (2003) *Identifying and Implementing Educational Practices Supported by Rigorous Evidence: A User Friendly Guide*, Washington,

DC: US Department of Education. Online. Available HTTP: <http://www.ed. gov/rschstat/research/pubs/rigorousevid/guide.html> (accessed 10 February 2005).

Viennot, L. (2001) *Reasoning in Physics: The Part of Common Sense*, Dordrecht, Netherlands: Kluwer.

Viennot, L. (2003) 'Relating research in didactics and actual teaching practice: Impact and virtues of critical details', in D. Psillos, P. Kariotoglou, V. Tselfes, E. Hatzikraniotis, G. Fassoulopoulos and M. Kallery (eds) *Science Education Research in the Knowledge-based Society*, Dordrecht, Netherlands: Kluwer.

Viennot, L. and Rainson, S. (1999) 'Design and evaluation of a research based teaching sequence: The superposition of electric fields', *International Journal of Science Education*, 21 (1): 1–16.

von Glaserfeld, E. (1995) *Radical Constructivism: A Way of Knowing and Learning*, London: Falmer Press.

Vosniadou, S. (1994) 'Capturing and modelling the process of conceptual change', *Learning and Instruction* 4: 45–69.

Vulliamy, G. (2004) 'The impact of globalisation on qualitative research in comparative and international education', *Compare*, 34 (3): 261–284.

Vygotsky, L.S. (1934) 'Thinking and speech', in R.W. Rieber and A.S. Carton (eds) (1987) *The Collected Works of L.S. Vygotsky*, trans. N. Minich, New York: Plenum Press.

Vygotsky, L.S. (1978) *Mind in Society: The Development of Higher Psychological Processes*, Cambridge, MA: Harvard University Press.

Webb, R., Vulliamy, G., Hämäläinen, S., Sarja, A., Kimonen, E. and Nevalainen, R. (2004) 'A comparative analysis of primary teacher professionalism in England and Finland, *Comparative Education*, 40 (1): 83–107.

Wenger, E. (1998) *Communities of Practice: Learning, Meaning and Identity*, New York: Cambridge University Press.

Wertsch, J.V. (1991) *Voices of the Mind: A Sociocultural Approach to Mediated Action*, Cambridge, MA: Harvard University Press.

What Works Clearinghouse (2003) *A Trusted Source of Evidence of What Works in Education*. Online. Available HTTP: <http://www.w-w-c.org/> (accessed 10 February 2005).

Index